More Praise for *Night of Beginnings*

A prophet and founding mother of feminist Judaism, Marcia Falk has played a pioneering role in modern Jewish ritual and liturgy. Immersed in profound knowledge of the traditional sources and a fresh vision of Jewish worship, her writing has inspired worshippers, writers, and religious leaders for over four decades. Her newest gift, *Night of Beginnings*, is a work of wisdom, art, and love.

—RABBI DALIA MARX, Professor of Liturgy, Hebrew Union College, Jerusalem

Marcia Falk has lovingly gifted us with a poetic recounting of the biblical narrative along with eloquent rituals, blessings, and meditations. Pastel-colored pages invite readers to distinguish the book's varied elements. Rather than illustrate her haggadah with yet more interpretations of centuries-old classic iconography, Falk adorns her celebratory text with her own elegantly drafted spring flora to create a gorgeous and exceptionally important haggadah.

—MARK PODWAL, artist, recipient of the Foundation for Jewish Culture Achievement Award

Every generation must see itself as leaving Egypt, and every generation must tell the story anew. In this resonant retelling, Marcia Falk weaves ancient passages with new poetic creations. Newcomers as well as those deeply engaged with Jewish ritual will discover the overflowing of Miriam's and Elijah's cups in this stunning haggadah.

—RABBI NAAMAH KELMAN, Dean, Hebrew Union College, Jerusalem

In *Night of Beginnings*, Marcia Falk continues the brilliant, groundbreaking work she began in her *Book of Blessings*. Her poetic voice seamlessly combines a profoundly feminist orientation with deep reading of Jewish tradition, and her sometimes daring *kavanot* (directions of the heart) encourage fresh conversation to renew the seder experience for contemporary participants.

—RABBI DAVID TEUTSCH, editor, *Kol Haneshamah* Reconstructionist prayer books

לילה של התחלות

NIGHT OF BEGINNINGS

ALSO BY MARCIA FALK

The Book of Blessings: New Jewish Prayers for Daily Life, the Sabbath, and the New Moon Festival
A re-creation of Hebrew and English liturgy from a nonhierarchical, inclusive perspective, with notes and commentary

The Days Between: Blessings, Poems, and Directions of the Heart for the Jewish High Holiday Season
A re-creation of Hebrew and English liturgy for Rosh Hashanah, Yom Kippur, and the days between them

Inner East: Illuminated Poems and Blessings
Poetry accompanied by the author's artwork

The Song of Songs: A New Translation and Interpretation
Translation from the Hebrew, with introduction, notes, and commentary

The Song of Songs: Love Lyrics from the Bible
Translation from the Hebrew, with introduction

With Teeth in the Earth: Selected Poems of Malka Heifetz Tussman
Translations from the Yiddish, with notes and introduction

The Spectacular Difference: Selected Poems of Zelda
Translations from the Hebrew, with notes and introduction

My Son Likes Weather
Poems

It Is July in Virginia
Poems

This Year in Jerusalem
Poems

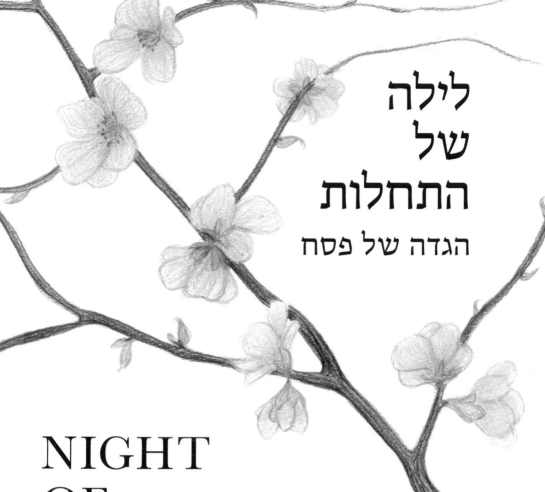

לילה
של
התחלות
הגדה של פסח

NIGHT
OF
BEGINNINGS

A PASSOVER HAGGADAH

Marcia Falk

With drawings by the author

The Jewish Publication Society
Philadelphia

University of Nebraska Press
Lincoln

Manufactured in the United States of America
Interior and cover design by Rachelle Vagy

Library of Congress
Control Number: 2021940091

for Steven Rood
חיים שיע

and

Abraham Gilead Falk-Rood
אברהם גילעד

as ever

CONTENTS

פתיחת החג
OPENING THE FESTIVAL

תחילת הסדר
BEGINNING THE SEDER

Contents

לקראת המגיד
BEFORE THE MAGGID: PREPARING TO LISTEN

מגיד
MAGGID: THE TELLING

אחרי המגיד
AFTER THE MAGGID: CELEBRATING THE STORY

סעודת החג
THE FESTIVAL MEAL

סיום
CONCLUDING THE SEDER

Contents

שירים
SONGS

INTRODUCTION

Walking through the walnut orchard,
Looking for the signs of spring:
The pomegranates—have they flowered?
The grapevines—are they blossoming?

SONG OF SONGS 6:11

A BOOK OF BEGINNINGS

Springtime: the world is budding, the earth is blossoming; why not we too? This is the time of openings, and tonight—the first night of Pesach—is a night of beginnings.

The book that you hold in your hands is a book of and about beginnings, in which you are invited to take part. On Pesach we celebrate two beginnings: the departure from Egypt—the first step in our becoming a free people—and the start of the year, which, in the Book of Exodus, takes place in the springtime month of *Aviv* (later called *Nisan*). Thus the earth's cycles and our people's journey from slavery to freedom overlap in the Festival of Spring, *Ḥag Ha'aviv*. (*Ḥag Ha'aviv* was one of the rabbis' names for Pesach. The eleventh-century rabbi Sh'lomo Yitzhaki, known as Rashi, comments that the season and the journey are purposefully intertwined: he praises God for timing the Exodus in the spring, when travel is least arduous.)

This haggadah itself is a new beginning. But why—why begin again? Why yet another new haggadah?

Meaning: it is always about meaning. The intention of *Night of Beginnings* is to do more than "update" the traditional liturgy, to do more than make it consonant with contemporary thinking and sensibilities. This haggadah is an attempt to go beyond these aims to reveal meanings beneath the surface of the Pesach ritual and to deepen our personal connections to the holiday.

FROM THEN TO NOW

Night of Beginnings is modeled on the basic structure and themes of the traditional haggadah, and, at the same time, it participates in the centuries-long history of transformation and adaptation that yielded today's *haggadot* (plural of haggadah). It may be helpful to take a brief moment to look at this long history.

The Pesach holiday has its origins in Tanakh (the Hebrew Bible) where, at God's command, Moshe instructs the Israelites to create a festival honoring God for sparing them the death of their firstborns and for liberating them from enslavement in Egypt. After the destruction of the Second Temple, the rabbis began to develop a ritual that could be enacted at the family table. From these earliest beginnings a version of the haggadah emerged and, over the course of many centuries, evolved. Not until well after the printing press was invented did the haggadah begin to resemble what we tend to think of today as the "standard" text (specifically, the Ashkenazic version from eastern Europe). But the history of its development shows that "tradition" was—and in fact still is—constantly being changed.

In our times, we have seen a profusion of different kinds of *haggadot*. And yet, strikingly, one is hard-pressed to find in any haggadah, ancient or modern, a full recounting of the biblical story. It is doubly ironic that, although the word-root of both *haggadah* and *Maggid* (the central portion of this haggadah) means "telling," the standard haggadah does not actually tell the Exodus story—in fact, it does not offer a continuous narrative at all. Instead, it provides tastings—rabbinic anecdotes, comments, and exhortations, punctuated with biblical quotations—that show us how the generations of rabbis who created and redacted the haggadah viewed the purpose and meaning of the Pesach festival and how they wanted us to view and observe it. For many of us, this compilation fails to engage the way that stories do and fails to draw us deeply into our own search for the festival's meaning.

In recounting the full Bible story, *Night of Beginnings* seeks to provide a more direct connection to the origins of the holiday. "Maggid: The Telling"— which is not only the centerpiece of this haggadah but one of its three main innovative elements—offers a compressed version of the Exodus narrative, beginning with the Israelites' enslavement and ending with their crossing the Sea of Reeds. Presented this way, the narrative is revealed to have a dramatic trajectory with an opening, a climax, and a denouement. No attempt has been made here to make the character of God gender-inclusive; in the Exodus story God is decidedly male, and it is this story that we investigate and seek to understand tonight, in all its complexity. Importantly, unlike the standard haggadah, which omits any mention of the story's main human protagonists, "Maggid: The Telling" includes the voices and actions not just of Moshe and his brother, Aaron, but of the female characters, among them Moshe's mother; his sister, Miriam; Pharaoh's daughter, who adopts the baby Moshe; and the midwives Shifrah and Pu'ah, who save the lives of Hebrew male infants.

Interspersed throughout the narration is a new commentary, indicated in **bold** letters, that raises questions of interpretation and invites us to bring our personal experiences into the discussion.

Besides "Maggid: The Telling," *Night of Beginnings* offers two other major innovations: new *b'rakhot* (plural of *b'rakhah*, blessing), which are re-creations, in Hebrew and in English, of the traditional blessings; and *kavanot* (plural of *kavanah*, intention, or direction of the heart), a genre that is entirely new to the seder ritual. (Each of these elements is set apart in the design of the book; see the notes for the reader, which follow this introduction.)

The new *b'rakhot* express a theology that differs distinctly from that of the traditional rabbinic blessings as well as from that of the Bible story. They envision the divine—the ineffable, the sacred—as a greater whole of which we are an inseparable part. They convey this vision with images—new metaphors, such as *eyn hahayim* (wellspring of life) and *ma'yan hayéynu* (flow of our lives)—that replace the depiction of God as a lord and king. These new metaphors are neither anthropomorphic (not male and not female) nor abstract, but drawn largely from the natural world. Their inclusive language makes room for women to find and use our voices more full-throatedly than we were able to do with the patriarchal prayers we inherited from the early rabbis.

In addition to offering new imagery, the *b'rakhot* differ from rabbinic prayer in their mode of address: rather than passively acknowledging a "blessed You," they open with inclusive, active verbs, such as *n'varekh* (let us bless) and *nodeh* (let us thank), calling upon us, the human community, to perform the act of blessing. Some of the *b'rakhot* open directly with an image, leaving the invocation implied. Each *b'rakhah* is introduced with a quotation from Tanakh, linking it to our most ancient texts. All the *b'rakhot* ask that we bring our attention to the fullness of the moment and, at times, that we commit to fulfilling the words of the blessing with action, not just ritually but in the acts of our ordinary daily lives. *B'rakhot* are the core of every seder ritual, as they are in this haggadah; simply put, without them there is no seder.

The *kavanot* in *Night of Beginnings* amplify the *b'rakhot*, and we might think of them as the seder's heart. Although they are innovations— they do not appear at all in the traditional ritual— they are founded on the rabbinic injunction to always bring something new to prayer; to pray, with intentionality, *hat'filah shebalev* (the prayer of the heart). If the *b'rakhot* are short lyric poems that touch down lightly on single moments—the lighting of candles, the eating of matzah—the *kavanot* take the form of longer prose-poems and meditations, inviting us to delve more deeply and broadly, lingering over images, themes, and motifs, and allowing ourselves to enter more fully and more personally into the experience of the night.

Interspersed among the three main innovative elements of this haggadah—the *b'rakhot*, the *kavanot*, and the Maggid—are several kinds of embellishments: poems, psalms, and songs, as well as traditional readings that are usually sung, including *Arba Hakushyot* (the Four Questions), *Sh'faḥot Va'avadim Hayinu* (Once We Were Slaves), *Ha Lahma Anya* (This Is the Bread of Affliction), *B'khol Dor Vador* (In Every Generation), and *Dayénu* (It Would Have Been Enough). All of these readings, with the exception of *Dayénu*, have been adapted to make them more inclusive. The traditional songs that follow the seder proper have, like *Dayénu*, been left unaltered for the sake of maintaining their "singability." In the words of Rabbi Ira Eisenstein *z"l*, we sing these "as quotation rather than affirmation." Some of the traditional readings have been moved from their usual places in the haggadah; rather than being scattered throughout, they are clustered in two sections that frame the Maggid: "Before the Maggid: Preparing to Listen" and "After the Maggid: Celebrating the Story." These modifications to the structure of the standard haggadah lend coherence to what has felt, to many people, like a less-than-unified creation.

CONCEALMENT, REVEALMENT, AND THE LANGUAGE OF POETRY

Underlying many aspects of *Night of Beginnings* is the motif of hidden-ness-and-uncovering. In "Maggid: The Telling," this motif is recurrent: Moshe starts life hidden in a basket in the Nile, and over the course of the narrative he becomes a prominent leader and a prophet. This progression from the concealed and inchoate to a revealed identity parallels the emergence of the Israelites from enslavement into peoplehood. So too, in Exodus 3 God reveals His heretofore hidden name— *Ehyeh-Asher-Ehyeh* (I Am That I Am)—to Moshe for the first time.

The framework of the seder ritual echoes this motif. Near the start of the seder, the leader hides the *afikoman* (a broken-off piece of matzah) and, toward the end of the meal, the *afikoman*—essential for concluding the seder—is found.

In an essay entitled "Revealment and Concealment in Language," the great twentieth-century Hebrew poet Hayim Nahman Bialik wrote of how language conceals truths and yet how, paradoxically, when crafted as poetry, language can reveal the hidden core of things. *Night of Beginnings* speaks, in large part, in the language of poetry—with *b'rakhot* and lyric poems created specially for the seder, *kavanot* that take the form of prose poems, biblical psalms, readings from the Song of Songs, and modern poems. This assemblage of poetic modes will, I hope, serve to uncover meanings and nuances that might otherwise be buried or obscured.

This is a poet's Passover, and as we read aloud from it, we all partake in poetry's power to reveal. In this sense, tonight we are all poets.

FREEDOM, THE SELF, AND OTHERS

The theme of concealment and revealment embedded in *Night of Beginnings* has implications for our personal attainment of freedom. Self-awareness—being revealed to oneself—is a necessary (though not sufficient) condition for freedom. The less one is hidden from oneself, the greater one's potential for self-actualization, the fruit of a freely chosen life.

And the greater one's freedom, the better one's ability to pursue freedom and justice in the world. Self-awareness is not just a necessary condition for personal freedom; it is the grounding of one's awareness of the needs of others—the first step in the journey out of the wilderness.

MAKING THIS NIGHT YOURS

Night of Beginnings will grow with you and your family and community. If young children are present, you might wish to omit some or all of the *kavanot*, which may be difficult for the children to grasp. Or you might omit the commentary in the Maggid. And if the Maggid is still too long for your purposes, you can choose to read the abbreviated version that follows the full version.

As the children attending the seder become teenagers and young adults, you may want to increase opportunities for discussion by bringing in some of the readings that you previously omitted. Whether or not children are present, you will have in your hands a resource for deep conversation.

It is my wish that this haggadah will open up meaningful new beginnings for you—new experiences of the Pesach holiday, new relationships to tradition, and, ideally, new insight into your personal potential for liberation.

NOTES FOR THE READER

TRANSLITERATIONS

Alongside the Hebrew passages in this volume, in italicized English letters, is a nonlanguage sometimes referred to as "transliteration." The system used here is neither perfectly scientific (that would be too clumsy to read) nor perfectly phonetic (that would be nearly impossible). Rather, it is intended to help English readers who know little or no Hebrew to approximate the sounds of the original and to recognize basic sentence structure through punctuation and capitalization. Because Hebrew has no capital letters, capitals appear in the transliteration only where they would appear in English for purposes of form and syntax (i.e., at the beginnings of sentences and in titles) and not to indicate proper names.

All words are stressed on the final syllable except those with accent marks, indicating penultimate or antepenultimate stress. Most consonants are pronounced as they would be in English. Note that "g" is hard, as in "gusto; "kh" is a guttural letter (the *khaf*), pronounced like the final consonant of "Bach"; "ḥ" represents another guttural (the letter *ḥet*), which is similar (but not identical) in pronunciation to the letter *khaf*.

The vowel sounds are "a" as in the first syllable of "matzah"; "e" as in "egg"; "i" as in either "pickle" or "teriyaki"; "o" as in either "corn" or "bone"; "u" as in "umami"; "ay" as in "papaya"; "ey" as in "whey." The letters *álef* and *áyin*, pronounced as glottal stops in modern Hebrew, are indicated by apostrophes when they appear in the middle of a word. Apostrophes also stand for the mobile *sh'va*, a very short vowel usually pronounced like the "a" in "pizza" or "spaghetti" (to be consumed post-Pesach, of course).

Like any system of rules, this one has its exceptions. A few Hebrew words that are familiar to many English readers and often go untranslated in Jewish contexts, such as *kiddush* and *shabbat*, are given in their common English spellings.

PROPER NAMES

Throughout the book, Passover is referred to by its anglicized Hebrew name, Pesach, except in passages transliterated from Hebrew, where it is spelled *pésaḥ*, according to the transliteration convention established here. Moses is called by his Hebrew name, Moshe. All other proper names, such as Miriam and Aaron, are given in their common anglicized versions.

TRANSLATIONS AND ADAPTATIONS

Translations from the Bible—including the Psalms, the biblical epigraphs to the blessings, and the passages quoted from the Book of Exodus in "Maggid: The Telling"—are my own, as are the translations from Talmud and Midrash. The layout and translation of the Song of Songs are from my book *The Song of Songs: Love Lyrics from the Bible* (Brandeis University Press, 2004).

I have translated the Psalms and the biblical epigraphs—which are, for the most part, poetic texts—with a degree of freedom that has included the expansion of names for the Divine. So too, my version of the Song of Songs takes liberties with the translation of the Hebrew, in an effort to capture the poetic qualities of this supremely lyrical book.

In contrast, in the case of the Book of Exodus, I have tried as much as possible to starkly convey the literal meaning of the text—especially regarding the Divine, which is always referred to in the Hebrew with male pronouns. My purpose in presenting the Exodus in a literal translation is to allow us to study the text as I believe it would have been understood at the time of its original composition.

Three rabbinic Hebrew and Aramaic texts—*Sh'faḥot Va'avadim Hayinu, Ha Laḥma Anya, and B'khol Dor Vador*—have been presented with alterations to make them more gender-inclusive. These adaptations are noted in the introductory comments to the passages, and their English counterparts reflect the adapted Hebrew text.

TINTED PAGES

To make the genres easily recognizable, tinted pages in the book have been matched to specific genres. The three main elements of the book appear as follows: **b'rakhot** (on apricot pages), **kavanot** (on blueberry pages), and the **Maggid** (on sage-green pages). Other color-keyed sections include **Spring Poems from the Song of Songs** (on raspberry pages) and **Hallel 1** and **Hallel 2** (on peach pages).

פתיחת החג

OPENING
THE FESTIVAL

הדלקת נרות חג הפסח

LIGHTING THE PESACH CANDLES

HADLAKAT NEROT ḤAG HAPÉSAḤ

THE CANDLES ARE LIT, AND THE BLESSING IS SAID.

LIGHTING THE PESACH CANDLES

The people who walked in darkness
have seen a great light.
For those who dwelt in death's shadow
a light has shone.

ISAIAH 9:1

May the lights of Pesach awaken
the light within
and reveal the way
to freedom.

הַדְלָקַת נֵרוֹת חַג הַפֶּסַח

הָעָם הַהֹלְכִים בַּחֹשֶׁךְ
רָאוּ אוֹר גָּדוֹל
יֹשְׁבֵי בְּאֶרֶץ צַלְמָוֶת
אוֹר נָגַהּ עֲלֵיהֶם.

ישעיהו ט:א

יָעִירוּ נֵרוֹת חַג הַפֶּסַח
אֶת הָאוֹר בְּקִרְבֵּנוּ
הַמֵּאִיר אֶת דַּרְכֵּנוּ
לְחֵרוּת.

*HADLAKAT NEROT
ḤAG HAPÉSAḤ*

*Ha'am hahol'khim baḥóshekh
ra'u or gadol
yosh'vey b'éretz tzalmávet
or nagah aleyhem.*

ISAIAH 9:1

*Ya'íru nerot ḥag hapésaḥ
et ha'or b'kirbénu
hame'ir et darkénu
l'ḥerut.*

3

ON SHABBAT, SUBSTITUTE THIS BLESSING.

LIGHTING THE SHABBAT
AND PESACH CANDLES

The people who walked in darkness
have seen a great light.
For those who dwelt in death's shadow
a light has shone.

ISAIAH 9:1

May the lights of Shabbat and Pesach
awaken the light within
and reveal the way
to freedom.

הַדְלָקַת נֵרוֹת הַשַׁבָּת וְחַג הַפֶּסַח

HADLAKAT NEROT HASHABBAT V'ḤAG HAPÉSAḤ

הָעָם הַהֹלְכִים בַּחֹשֶׁךְ
רָאוּ אוֹר גָּדוֹל
יֹשְׁבֵי בְּאֶרֶץ צַלְמָוֶת
אוֹר נָגַהּ עֲלֵיהֶם.

ישעיהו ט:א

Ha'am hahol'khim baḥóshekh
ra'u or gadol
yosh'vey b'éretz tzalmávet
or nagah aleyhem.

ISAIAH 9:1

יָעִירוּ נֵרוֹת הַשַׁבָּת וְחַג הַפֶּסַח
אֶת הָאוֹר בְּקִרְבֵּנוּ
הַמֵּאִיר אֶת דַּרְכֵּנוּ
לְחֵרוּת.

Ya'íru nerot hashabbat v'ḥag hapésaḥ
et ha'or b'kirbénu
hame'ir et darkénu
l'ḥerut.

THE JOURNEY: LIGHTING THE WAY
KAVANAH

Day turns to night: the festival begins. Day turns to night again: the festival ends. We light candles to mark both turnings.

We light—and we distinguish between weekdays and holy days. So every holiday and every Sabbath begin with candlelighting. And the ritual that ends holidays and Sabbaths, which is marked by the lighting of a multi-wicked candle, is called *havdalah* (distinctions). Without the week, there is no Sabbath. If every day were a holiday, "holiday" would have no meaning.

But lighting candles is not just about making distinctions; it is also about connection, the meeting place between one being and another. Light takes us across the boundaries. We light the way, and we find our way: the sea parts, and we cross to the other side.

The symbol of light is never more apt than on Pesach, when we mark our crossing from Egypt—the place of our exile and enslavement—to Canaan, the place we would come to call home. The word *ivrim* (Hebrews), another name for the Israelites, is related to *avar*, meaning "cross over." Tonight we are all *ivrim*. As we tell the story of our flight from Egypt, we cross boundaries not only of space but of time. As we recount, we re-enact with all our senses—tasting, smelling, hearing, seeing, and touching—ushering the past into the present moment.

ברכת הזמן

BLESSING OF TIME AND RENEWAL

BIRKAT HAZ'MAN (SHEHEḤEYÁNU)

BLESSING OF TIME AND RENEWAL

Springs gush in the riverbeds,
flowing between the hills.

PSALM 104:10

Let us bless the flow of life
that revives us,
sustains us,
and brings us to this time.

בִּרְכַּת הַזְּמַן

הַמְשַׁלֵּחַ מַעְיָנִים בַּנְּחָלִים
בֵּין הָרִים יְהַלֵּכוּן.

תהלים קד:י

BIRKAT HAZ'MAN

Hamshalé'ah má'yanim ban'halim
beyn harim y'halekhun.

PSALM 104:10

נְבָרֵךְ אֶת מַעְיָן חַיֵּינוּ
שֶׁהֶחֱיָנוּ
וְקִיְּמָנוּ
וְהִגִּיעָנוּ לַזְּמַן הַזֶּה.

N'varekh et ma'yan hayéynu
sheheheyánu
v'kiy'mánu
v'higi'ánu laz'man hazeh.

9

CHANGE: THE FLOW OF LIFE
KAVANAH

Here we are, once again, about to recount the transformative story of our peoplehood—just as we did last year, and the year before. Every year we tell the same story, but each year we are enjoined to make it new, to bring our own lives into it, to view it as if it had happened to each of us individually. Repetition and newness: together they are the flow.

The fountain, the flow of life. All life, forever in motion, ever renewing and being renewed. History is movement, and movement is change. With the "Blessing of Time and Renewal"—in Hebrew, *Birkat Haz'man* (the blessing of time)—we bring to awareness the passing of time and the passages that time has brought us through. We welcome the moment in which we stand, even as we see ourselves moving forward.

As we renew the festival, we renew our selves, immersing ourselves in the flow of time—the flow of life.

ברכת הבת, ברכת הבן
BLESSING THE CHILDREN
BIRKAT HABAT, BIRKAT HABEN

THIS BLESSING MAY BE GIVEN BY PARENTS TO THEIR CHILDREN (OF ANY AGE) OR BY ADULTS TO YOUNGER PEOPLE AT THE TABLE.

BLESSING THE CHILDREN

The squares of the city will be filled
with boys and girls playing.

ZECHARIAH 8:5

[The child's name]—
Be who you are,
and may you be blessed
in all that you are.

בִּרְכַּת הַבַּת

וּרְחֹבוֹת הָעִיר יִמָּלְאוּ יְלָדִים וִילָדוֹת
מְשַׂחֲקִים בִּרְחֹבֹתֶיהָ.

זכריה ח:ה

[שֵׁם הַבַּת]—
הֲיִי אֲשֶׁר תִּהְיִי
וַהֲיִי בְּרוּכָה
בַּאֲשֶׁר תִּהְיִי.

BIRKAT HABAT

*Urhovot ha'ir yimal'u y'ladim viladot
m'sahakim birhovotéha.*

ZECHARIAH 8:5

[The girl's name]—
*Hayi asher tihyi
vahayi b'rukhah
ba'asher tihyi.*

בִּרְכַּת הַבֵּן

וּרְחֹבוֹת הָעִיר יִמָּלְאוּ יְלָדִים וִילָדוֹת
מְשַׂחֲקִים בִּרְחֹבֹתֶיהָ.

זכריה ח:ה

[שֵׁם הַבֵּן]—
הֱיֵה אֲשֶׁר תִּהְיֶה
וֶהֱיֵה בָּרוּךְ
בַּאֲשֶׁר תִּהְיֶה.

BIRKAT HABEN

*Urhovot ha'ir yimal'u y'ladim viladot
m'sahakim birhovotéha.*

ZECHARIAH 8:5

[The boy's name]—
*Hehyey asher tihyeh
vehehyey barukh
ba'asher tihyeh.*

תחילת הסדר

BEGINNING
THE SEDER

THE SEDER PLATE

THE LEADER EXPLAINS THE SYMBOLS ON THE SEDER PLATE AND AT THE TABLE.

Z'ro'a / Roasted shank bone, representing the lamb that was offered as a sacrifice on the Israelites' first night of freedom (some households substitute a broiled beet)

Betzah / Roasted egg, symbolizing, in ancient agricultural festivals, new births and renewals of spring; later also becoming a symbol of the sacrificial offering in the Pesach festival

Maror / Horseradish root (the word-root of *maror* means "bitter") to remind us of the bitterness of our lives in Egypt

Haróset / Sweet nut-and-fruit paste, prepared with varying recipes in different communities, to suggest the appearance of the mortar or clay used for making bricks in Egypt

Karpas / Parsley or other greens, a sign of spring

Hazéret / Lettuce or another bitter vegetable (optional), an additional symbol of bitterness

THE SEDER TABLE

The key symbol of Pesach is matzah, unleavened bread (plural *matzot*). In the Bible, Pesach is called *Ḥag Hamatzot*, the "Festival of *Matzot*."

Ancient Israelites brought sheaves of the new grain, unprocessed and unleavened, to the Temple as the first offering of the agricultural cycle. This ritual predates the mythological association of matzah with the Exodus from Egypt.

In the biblical context, matzah has a double meaning. In Deuteronomy 16:3, it is referred to as *léḥem óni*, "the bread of affliction (or poverty, or distress)"—the food we ate while enslaved. But in the same passage we are told that we are to eat matzah because it reminds us of our hurried flight from Egypt, when we did not have time to wait for the bread to rise. Thus, although matzah—*léḥem óni*—symbolizes our oppression, in the context of the story it is also the bread of freedom, sustaining us as we fled from bondage.

The matzah is not placed on the seder plate; rather, three *matzot* are stacked on the table, separated by cloths. A little later in the seder, the leader will break the middle matzah in half and put the larger half, called the *afikoman*, aside, to be hidden and then found toward the end of the meal.

A cup of wine is set on the table for the prophet Elijah. In the last part of the seder, we will invite Elijah into our midst.

We place a dish of saltwater on the table. Later in the seder we will dip the spring greens in the saltwater to symbolize the tears of our ancestors.

In recent years, many new symbols have been added to the seder table, representing issues of current concern (such as racism, homophobia, climate change, mass incarceration, human trafficking, and the plight of refugees and asylum-seekers). Perhaps the most well-known symbol of our times is *Kos Miryam* (Miriam's Cup), a goblet filled with spring water, which was introduced in the late twentieth century by Jewish feminists to call to mind and celebrate women's places in the tradition. Miriam plays a crucial role in the Exodus narrative, as we will see when we read the Maggid portion of the haggadah. We place Miriam's cup in a central spot on the table. After the Maggid, we say a special blessing for *Kos Miryam*.

By far the most important symbol at the table is the community of participants. Whether two people or thirty are in attendance, tonight we represent *am yisra'el*, the people of Israel.

קדש ורחץ

ORDER OF THE NIGHT

(KADESH URḤATZ)

The word *seder* means "order"; *Kadesh Urḥatz* is a mnemonic for remembering the traditional order of key blessings and ritual acts in the seder. It is usually sung, in Hebrew. The English translation that appears below is for reference rather than for singing.

THE WINE CUPS ARE FILLED, AND WE SING THE HEBREW WORDS.

Sanctification *(kiddush)*	Kadesh	קַדֵּשׁ
Washing the Hands *(without a blessing)*	Urḥatz	וּרְחַץ
Spring Greens	Karpas	כַּרְפַּס
Breaking *(of the middle piece of matzah)*	Yáhatz	יַחַץ
The Telling	Maggid	מַגִּיד
Washing the Hands *(with a blessing)*	Rohtzah	רָחְצָה
Blessing before the Meal,	Motzi'ah,	מוֹצִיאָה,
Blessing for Eating Matzah	Matzah	מַצָּה
Bitter Herb	Maror	מָרוֹר
Hillel Sandwich *(bitter herb and matzah)*	Korekh	כּוֹרֵךְ
Setting the Table *(the meal)*	Shulḥan Orekh	שֻׁלְחָן עוֹרֵךְ
Hidden *(the afikoman)*	Tzafun	צָפוּן
Blessing after the Meal	Barekh	בָּרֵךְ
Hallel (psalms and poems of praise)	Hallel	הַלֵּל
Fulfillment *(concluding the seder)*	Nirtzah	נִרְצָה

קדש

SANCTIFICATION (KIDDUSH)

KADESH

WE DRINK FOUR CUPS OF WINE DURING THE COURSE OF THE SEDER; THE FIRST IS A *KIDDUSH*, A SANCTIFICATION OF THE HOLIDAY. WE FILL THE WINE CUPS, SAY THE BLESSING, AND DRINK.

FRUIT OF THE VINE, HALLOWING THE DAY

Wine refreshes those
who are weary in the wilderness.

2 SAMUEL 16:2

On this Festival of Freedom, we cross
from wilderness to promise,

from exile to home,
from enslavement to fully lived lives.

We hallow this day and bless
the ever-flowing wellspring,

which sustains us on the way,
nourishing the fruit of the vines.

בִּרְכַּת פְּרִי הַגֶּפֶן,
קְדֻשַּׁת הַיּוֹם

וְהַיַּיִן לִשְׁתּוֹת הַיָּעֵף בַּמִּדְבָּר.

שמואל ב, טז:ב

בְּחַג הַחֵרוּת הַזֶּה,
נַעֲבֹר מִמִּדְבָּר לְתִקְוָה,

מִגָּלוּת לְבַיִת,
מֵעַבְדוּת לְחַיִּים שְׁלֵמִים.

נְקַדֵּשׁ יוֹם זֶה, וּנְבָרֵךְ
אֶת הַמַּעְיָן הַשּׁוֹפֵעַ

הַמְחַיֵּנוּ בַּדֶּרֶךְ
וּמַרְוֶה אֶת פְּרִי הַגֶּפֶן.

**BIRKAT P'RI HAGÉFEN,
K'DUSHAT HAYOM**

*V'hayáyin lishtot
haya'ef bamidbar.*

2 SAMUEL 16:2

*B'ḥag haḥerut hazeh,
na'avor mimidbar l'tikvah,*

*migalut l'váyit,
me'avdut l'ḥayim sh'lemim.*

*N'kadesh yom zeh, unvarekh
et hama'yan hashofé'a*

*hamḥayéynu badérekh
umarveh et p'ri hagéfen.*

23

ON SHABBAT, SUBSTITUTE THIS BLESSING.

FRUIT OF THE VINE,
HALLOWING THE DAY

Wine refreshes those
who are weary in the wilderness.

2 SAMUEL 16:2

On this Shabbat and Festival of Freedom,
we cross from wilderness to promise,

from exile to home,
from enslavement to fully lived lives.

We hallow this day and bless
the ever-flowing wellspring,

which sustains us on the way,
nourishing the fruit of the vines.

בִּרְכַּת פְּרִי הַגֶּפֶן,
קְדֻשַּׁת הַיּוֹם

BIRKAT P'RI HAGÉFEN,
K'DUSHAT HAYOM

וְהַיַּיִן לִשְׁתּוֹת הַיָּעֵף בַּמִּדְבָּר.
שמואל ב, טז:ב

V'hayáyin lishtot haya'ef bamidbar.

2 SAMUEL 16:2

בְּשַׁבָּת הַזֹּאת
וְחַג הַחֵרוּת הַזֶּה,
נַעֲבֹר מִמִּדְבָּר לְתִקְוָה,

Bashabbat hazot
v'ḥag haḥerut hazeh,
na'avor mimidbar l'tikvah,

מִגָּלוּת לְבַיִת,
מֵעַבְדוּת לְחַיִּים שְׁלֵמִים.

migalut l'váyit,
me'avdut l'ḥayim sh'lemim.

נְקַדֵּשׁ יוֹם זֶה, וּנְבָרֵךְ
אֶת הַמַּעְיָן הַשּׁוֹפֵעַ

N'kadesh yom zeh, unvarekh
et hama'yan hashofé'a

הַמְחַיֵּנוּ בַּדֶּרֶךְ
וּמַרְוֶה אֶת פְּרִי הַגֶּפֶן.

hamḥayéynu badérekh
umarveh et p'ri hagéfen.

25

FRUIT OF THE VINE
KAVANAH

The vine is tenacious, growing toward light without knowing what darkness may lie beyond. As it makes its way, it grows stronger, intertwining with other vines. In time, it will fruit; and the fruit will ripen and be sweet.

And so with us: as we set out on our individual paths, often unaware of our ultimate destinations, we find strength in the intersection of our lives with the lives and destinies of others. Community arises, sustaining and nourishing, as we seek to find our way.

The fruit of the vine is life, lived to its fullest potential.

The fruit of the vine is a life of freedom, meaning, and fulfillment.

ורחץ

WASHING THE HANDS

URḤATZ

WE PASS AROUND THE TABLE A PITCHER OF WATER, A BOWL, AND A
TOWEL, FOR WASHING THE HANDS. NO BLESSING IS SAID. (A BLESSING
WILL BE SAID FOR THE SECOND HANDWASHING, *ROḤTZAH*, WHICH
OCCURS AT THE START OF THE MEAL.)

כרפס

SPRING GREENS

KARPAS

In the Book of Exodus, the new year begins in the spring. When God instructs the Israelites on the celebration of the Pesach Festival, they are enjoined to mark the beginning of their calendar with their deliverance from Egypt: "This month [*Aviv*, springtime] shall mark for you the beginning of the months; it shall be the first of the months of the year for you" (Exodus 12:2). With *Karpas*—spring greens—we celebrate the flowering of the earth along with the birth of the year. There is also a darker aspect to the ritual of *Karpas*: dipping the greens in saltwater, we recall the tears of our enslaved ancestors.

WE DIP A SPRIG OF PARSLEY OR OTHER GREENS IN SALTWATER, SAY THE BLESSING, AND EAT.

DIPPING AND EATING
THE SPRING GREENS

> The vine shall give forth its fruit,
> the earth will yield its harvest,
> and the skies shall provide their dew.
>
> ZECHARIAH 8:12

At this Festival of Spring,
as we welcome the newly budding year,
let us bless the source that awakens
the greening of the earth.

30

טְבִילַת כַּרְפַּס
וַאֲכִילָתוֹ

הַגֶּפֶן תִּתֵּן פִּרְיָהּ
וְהָאָרֶץ תִּתֵּן אֶת־יְבוּלָהּ
וְהַשָּׁמַיִם יִתְּנוּ טַלָּם.

זכריה ח:יב

בְּחַג הָאָבִיב הַזֶּה
נְקַבֵּל אֶת פְּנֵי הַשָּׁנָה
וּנְבָרֵךְ אֶת הַמַּעְיָן הַמְּעוֹרֵר
אֶת פְּרִיחַת הָאָרֶץ.

T'VILAT KARPAS
VA'AKHILATO

Hagéfen titen piryah
v'ha'áretz titen et-y'vulah
v'hashamáyim yit'nu talam.

ZECHARIAH 8:12

B'ḥag ha'aviv hazeh
n'kabel et p'ney hashanah
unvarekh et hama'yan ham'orer
et p'riḥat ha'áretz.

SPRING: THE BIRTH OF THE YEAR
KAVANAH

We measure time in lines— forward and back. The story we recount at the seder table brings us back to ancient times: after years of enslavement, we leave Egypt to begin our journey to the Promised Land. At the same seder, we look to the future, to a time when the world will be redeemed and all will be free.

And we also measure time in cycles—birthdays and memorial days, monthly and yearly holidays, the weekly return of the Sabbath. Spring and fall, and spring again. We count the cycles not from beginning to end but from beginning to beginning: season begets season, month begets month, day begets day, without pause.

So Pesach comes, and goes, each year, always bringing with it something new: although the narrative we tell is the same, the way we view and understand it changes each time we tell it.

And each spring—each Pesach season—we encounter newness in the world around us and within us: new births, new blossoming, new beginnings.

שירי אביב
ממגילת שיר השירים

SPRING POEMS
FROM THE SONG OF SONGS

SHIREY AVIV
MIM'GILAT SHIR HASHIRIM

IT IS CUSTOMARY TO CHANT THE SONG OF SONGS, THE LOVE POETRY
OF THE BIBLE, ON THE SHABBAT OF PESACH. AN ESPECIALLY MUSICAL
COMPILATION, THE SONG OF SONGS HAS, OVER THE CENTURIES, BEEN
SET TO MANY MELODIES. TONIGHT WE READ—OR SING—EXCERPTS
PORTRAYING THE LUSHNESS OF THE SPRING SEASON.

Come with me,
my love,
come away

For the long wet months are past,
the rains have fed the earth
and left it bright with blossoms

Birds wing in the low skies,
dove and songbird singing
in the open air above

Earth nourishing tree and vine,
green fig and tender grape,
green and tender fragrance

Come with me,
my love,
come away

SONG OF SONGS 2:10–13

Anah dodi v'ámar li:

עָנָה דוֹדִי וְאָמַר לִי

Kúmi lakh ra'yati
yafati ulkhi-lakh.

קוּמִי לָךְ רַעְיָתִי
יָפָתִי וּלְכִי־לָךְ.

Ki-hiney has'tav avar
hagéshem ḥalaf halakh lo.

כִּי־הִנֵּה הַסְּתָו עָבָר
הַגֶּשֶׁם חָלַף הָלַךְ לוֹ.

Hanitzanim nir'u va'áretz
et hazamir higi'a
v'kol hator nishma b'artzénu.

הַנִּצָּנִים נִרְאוּ בָאָרֶץ
עֵת הַזָּמִיר הִגִּיעַ
וְקוֹל הַתּוֹר נִשְׁמַע בְּאַרְצֵנוּ.

Hat'enah ḥan'tah fagéha
v'hag'fanim s'madar nát'nu réyaḥ.

הַתְּאֵנָה חָנְטָה פַגֶּיהָ
וְהַגְּפָנִים סְמָדַר נָתְנוּ רֵיחַ.

Kúmi lakh ra'yati
yafati ulkhi-lakh.

קוּמִי לָךְ רַעְיָתִי
יָפָתִי וּלְכִי־לָךְ.

שיר השירים ב:י–יג

37

Turning to him, who meets me with desire—

Come, love, let us go out to the open fields
And spend our night lying where the henna blooms,
Rising early to leave for the near vineyards
Where the vines flower, opening tender buds,
And the pomegranate boughs unfold their blossoms.

There among blossom and vine I will give you my love,
Musk of the violet mandrakes spilled upon us . . .
And returning, finding our doorways piled with fruits,
The best of the new-picked and the long-stored,
My love, I will give you all I have saved for you.

SONG OF SONGS 7:11–14

Walking through the walnut orchard,
Looking for the signs of spring:
The pomegranates—have they flowered?
The grapevines—are they blossoming?

SONG OF SONGS 6:11

Ani l'dodi v'alay t'shukato.

אֲנִי לְדוֹדִי וְעָלַי תְּשׁוּקָתוֹ.

L'kha dodi netzey hasadeh
nalínah bak'farim.
Nashkimah lak'ramim
nir'eh im par'ḥah hagéfen
pitaḥ has'madar
henétzu harimonim.

לְכָה דוֹדִי נֵצֵא הַשָּׂדֶה
נָלִינָה בַּכְּפָרִים.
נַשְׁכִּימָה לַכְּרָמִים
נִרְאֶה אִם־פָּרְחָה הַגֶּפֶן
פִּתַּח הַסְּמָדַר
הֵנֵצוּ הָרִמּוֹנִים.

Sham eten et-doday lakh.
Haduda'im nat'nu-réyaḥ
v'al-p'taḥéynu kol-m'gadim
ḥadashim gam-y'shanim
dodi tzafánti lakh.

שָׁם אֶתֵּן אֶת־דֹּדַי לָךְ.
הַדּוּדָאִים נָתְנוּ־רֵיחַ
וְעַל־פְּתָחֵינוּ כָּל־מְגָדִים
חֲדָשִׁים גַּם־יְשָׁנִים
דּוֹדִי צָפַנְתִּי לָךְ.

שיר השירים ז:יא–יד

El-ginat egoz yaradti
lir'ot b'ibey hánaḥal
lir'ot hafar'ḥa hagéfen
henétzu harimonim.

אֶל־גִּנַּת אֱגוֹז יָרַדְתִּי
לִרְאוֹת בְּאִבֵּי הַנָּחַל
לִרְאוֹת הֲפָרְחָה הַגֶּפֶן
הֵנֵצוּ הָרִמֹּנִים.

שיר השירים ו:יא

39

In sandy earth or deep
In valley soil
I grow, a wildflower thriving
On your love.

Narcissus in the brambles,
Brightest flower—
I choose you from all others
For my love.

Sweet fruit tree growing wild
Within the thickets—
I blossom in your shade
And taste your love.

SONG OF SONGS 2:1–3

Ani ḥavatzélet hasharon
shoshanat ha'amakim.

אֲנִי חֲבַצֶּלֶת הַשָּׁרוֹן
שׁוֹשַׁנַּת הָעֲמָקִים.

K'shoshanah beyn haḥoḥim
ken ra'yati beyn habanot.

כְּשׁוֹשַׁנָּה בֵּין הַחוֹחִים
כֵּן רַעְיָתִי בֵּין הַבָּנוֹת.

K'tapú'aḥ ba'atzey hayá'ar
ken dodi beyn habanim.

כְּתַפּוּחַ בַּעֲצֵי הַיַּעַר
כֵּן דּוֹדִי בֵּין הַבָּנִים.

B'tzilo ḥimádti v'yashávti
ufiryo matok l'ḥiki.

בְּצִלּוֹ חִמַּדְתִּי וְיָשַׁבְתִּי
וּפִרְיוֹ מָתוֹק לְחִכִּי.

שיר השירים ב:א–ג

41

Enclosed and hidden, you are a garden,
A still pool, a fountain.

Stretching your limbs, you open—
A field of pomegranates blooms,

Treasured fruit among the blossoms,
Henna, sweet cane, bark, and saffron,

Fragrant woods and succulents,
The finest spices and perfumes.

Living water, you are a fountain,
A well, a river flowing from the mountains.

Come, north winds and south winds!
Breathe upon my garden,

Bear its fragrance to my lover,
Let him come and share its treasures.

My bride, my sister, I have come
To gather spices in my garden,

To taste wild honey with my wine,
Milk and honey with my wine.

Feast, drink—and drink deeply—lovers!

SONG OF SONGS 4:12–16; 5:1

Gan na'ul aḥoti khalah
gal na'ul ma'yan ḥatum.

גַּן נָעוּל אֲחֹתִי כַלָּה
גַּל נָעוּל מַעְיָן חָתוּם.

Sh'laḥáyikh pardes rimonim
im p'ri m'gadim
k'farim im-n'radim.

שְׁלָחַיִךְ פַּרְדֵּס רִמּוֹנִים
עִם פְּרִי מְגָדִים
כְּפָרִים עִם־נְרָדִים.

Nérd v'kharkom kaneh v'kinamon
im kol-atzey l'vonah
mor va'ahalot
im kol-rashey v'samim.

נֵרְדְּ וְכַרְכֹּם קָנֶה וְקִנָּמוֹן
עִם כָּל־עֲצֵי לְבוֹנָה
מֹר וַאֲהָלוֹת
עִם כָּל־רָאשֵׁי בְשָׂמִים.

Ma'yan ganim b'er máyim ḥayim
v'noz'lim min-l'vanon.

מַעְיַן גַּנִּים בְּאֵר מַיִם חַיִּים
וְנֹזְלִים מִן־לְבָנוֹן.

Úri tzafon uvó'i teyman
hafíḥi gani yiz'lu v'samav

עוּרִי צָפוֹן וּבוֹאִי תֵימָן
הָפִיחִי גַנִּי יִזְּלוּ בְשָׂמָיו

yavo dodi l'gano
v'yokhal p'ri m'gadav.

יָבֹא דוֹדִי לְגַנּוֹ
וְיֹאכַל פְּרִי מְגָדָיו.

Báti l'gani aḥoti khalah
aríti mori im-b'sami

בָּאתִי לְגַנִּי אֲחֹתִי כַלָּה
אָרִיתִי מוֹרִי עִם־בְּשָׂמִי

akhálti ya'ri im-divshi
shatíti yeyni im-ḥalavi.

אָכַלְתִּי יַעְרִי עִם־דִּבְשִׁי
שָׁתִיתִי יֵינִי עִם־חֲלָבִי.

Ikhlu re'im
sh'tu v'shikhru dodim.

אִכְלוּ רֵעִים
שְׁתוּ וְשִׁכְרוּ דּוֹדִים.

שִׁיר הַשִּׁירִים ד:יב־טז; ה:א

יחץ
BREAKING THE MATZAH, HIDING THE *AFIKOMAN*
YÁḤATZ

THE LEADER BREAKS THE MIDDLE MATZAH AND HIDES THE LARGER HALF, THE *AFIKOMAN*—THE START OF A TREASURE HUNT TO BE PLAYED BY THE CHILDREN. (IF THERE ARE NO CHILDREN AT THE SEDER, THE GROWN-UPS MUST PLAY.)

NEAR THE END OF THE SEDER, IN *TZAFUN*, "HIDDEN," THE CAPTURED *AFIKOMAN* WILL BE FOUND AND RETURNED.

BROKENNESS AND WHOLENESS
KAVANAH

Loss, suffering, hopelessness: broken spirit, broken self. Our lives are broken off by death. The human condition is brokenness.

But there is also another kind of breaking, the breaking-open of the heart that puts us in touch with our deeper selves and that may even serve as a gateway to wholeness.

What is wholeness of self? Does it depend on outer connections—bonds between self and other, between self and world? Is it the feeling that one is part of a greater whole?

Or is it an inner connectedness? An awareness, a knowing-ness sustained from within, a bringing forth to consciousness the hidden parts of the self? And might this deepened consciousness offer a path to freedom?

Or is wholeness all these things—and perhaps more?

We dwell in a world of brokenness, but we yearn and strive for wholeness. It is elusive, but it is our birthright.

The pursuit of wholeness is the human calling.

לקראת המגיד

BEFORE THE MAGGID:
PREPARING TO LISTEN

ארבע הקושיות

THE FOUR QUESTIONS

ARBA HAKUSHYOT

We are told that the main purpose of recounting the Exodus story is to teach the next generation—and all teaching begins with questions, spoken or unspoken. Questions are what give a teaching its relevance, its grip.

Here are the questions at the heart of the seder, the four questions that ask why this night is different. What follows them in the Maggid is the story that offers answers, the story through which we uncover the festival's meanings.

WE FILL THE WINE CUPS FOR A SECOND TIME. THE FOUR QUESTIONS
ARE SUNG—IDEALLY BY THE YOUNGEST PERSON PRESENT (NO
PRESSURE!).

THE FOUR QUESTIONS

Why is this night different
from all other nights?

On all other nights
we eat leavened and unleavened bread.
On this night—only matzah.

On all other nights
we eat all varieties of vegetables.
On this night—bitter herbs.

On all other nights
not even once do we dip (our food).
On this night—twice.

On all other nights
we eat either sitting up or reclining.
On this night—we recline.

אַרְבַּע הַקֻּשְׁיוֹת

מָה נִשְׁתַּנָּה הַלַּיְלָה הַזֶּה
מִכָּל הַלֵּילוֹת?

ARBA HAKUSHYOT

Mah nishtanah haláylah hazeh
mikol halelot?

שֶׁבְּכָל הַלֵּילוֹת אָנוּ אוֹכְלִין
חָמֵץ וּמַצָּה,
הַלַּיְלָה הַזֶּה כֻּלּוֹ מַצָּה.

שֶׁבְּכָל הַלֵּילוֹת אָנוּ אוֹכְלִין
שְׁאָר יְרָקוֹת,
הַלַּיְלָה הַזֶּה מָרוֹר.

Sheb'khol halelot ánu okhlin
hametz umatzah,
haláylah hazeh kulo matzah.

שֶׁבְּכָל הַלֵּילוֹת אֵין אָנוּ מַטְבִּילִין
אֲפִלּוּ פַּעַם אֶחָת,
הַלַּיְלָה הַזֶּה שְׁתֵּי פְעָמִים.

Sheb'khol halelot ánu okhlin
sh'ar y'rakot,
haláylah hazeh maror.

שֶׁבְּכָל הַלֵּילוֹת אָנוּ אוֹכְלִין
בֵּין יוֹשְׁבִין וּבֵין מְסֻבִּין,
הַלַּיְלָה הַזֶּה כֻּלָּנוּ מְסֻבִּין.

Sheb'khol halelot eyn ánu matbilin
afílu pá'am ehat,
haláylah hazeh sh'tey f'amim.

Sheb'khol halelot ánu okhlin
beyn yoshvin uveyn m'subin,
haláylah hazeh kulánu m'subin.

THE FOUR CHILDREN

The rabbis of the Talmud enjoin us to adapt our teaching to the one who asks the question. They speak of four types of questioners, four archetypal children (in the rabbis' eyes, sons): the wise one, the wicked one, the simple one, and the one who does not know how to ask. The monikers themselves reveal much about the rabbis' view of the world, as do the instructions the rabbis provide for teaching each child.

Here is what the rabbis tell us:

> The wise son asks for information; he (for the rabbis, the students are always male) is to be instructed in details of the law.

> The wicked son asks what the holiday means to you—which the rabbis view as meaning "to *you*—and not to himself." They see this child as excluding himself from the community, and therefore he is to be chastised, scorned, and shamed. He is to be told that had he been among the Israelites in Egypt, he would not have been liberated.

> The simple son asks a simple question, to which we are to offer a one-sentence summary of the Exodus story: "With a strong hand, God brought us out of Egypt, from the house of bondage."

To the son who does not know how to ask, we make our own assumptions and plunge in with our answer. We do not pause to consider what unspoken questions might be hidden within him.

To many of us today, the rabbis' archetypes are problematic and unhelpful. What might it be like if instead we were to view these children, of all genders, not as descriptions of separate individuals outside ourselves but as different parts of our selves *existing together within us*—within each of us? How might our replies be different?

WE READ THIS RE-VISIONING OF THE RABBIS' FOUR CHILDREN.
READERS MAY CHOOSE THEIR PREFERRED PRONOUNS.

Four children dwell within us:

THE CHILD WHO WANTS TO KNOW

The child who wants to know has an inquisitive mind and an open heart. When she asks "what?" and "how?" she wants to hear the whole story.

To this child you give full answers, because nothing less will do. When you don't know what to say, you keep looking. This child brings you the world.

THE CHILD WHO FEELS APART AND ALONE

There is another child who is hungry for truth, but of a different kind: he wants to know more about *you*; he asks what this holiday means *to you*. This child too is studying the world—*your* world. He is trying to find himself in you, through you.

Don't turn him away; let him cross your borders. He will bring you insight and surprise.

THE SIMPLE CHILD

The simple child asks the question that goes straight to the heart, stripping away pretense and complication. "What *is* this?" they ask. When the other children have finished their questioning, the simple child persists, asking, "Why?"

The simple child's question may be the most difficult one to answer. Nevertheless, try. This is the child who moves us on; this is the one who will change the world.

THE CHILD WHO CANNOT ASK

And then there is the child who cannot ask. She is cloaked in wonder; her voice is silence. She is who we were once—*before*. She hasn't left us, but she is often hidden, and we find her at unpredictable times.

We cannot call this child to us with words. She comes unbidden and, when she comes, the world reveals itself, suffused in beauty—beauty of which we are a part.

Bless this moment, bless this child. Nothing more to do. Blessed be the child beyond all questions.

שפחות ועבדים היינו

ONCE WE WERE SLAVES

SH'FAḤOT VA'AVADIM HAYÍNU

The rabbis begin their reply to the Four Questions by calling out the essence of the story—our enslavement in Egypt and our Exodus:

We were slaves to Pharaoh in Egypt, and God led us out with a mighty hand and an outstretched arm. Had our ancestors not been led out of Egypt, we and our children, and our children's children, would still be enslaved to Pharaoh in Egypt. Even if we were all wise, all of us sages, all of us advanced in age and learned in Torah, we would still be obliged to tell the story of the Exodus from Egypt. And the more the story is told, the better!

WE SING THESE HEBREW LINES. (A FEW WORDS HAVE BEEN ADDED TO
THE TRADITIONAL VERSION TO MAKE THE PASSAGE MORE GENDER-
INCLUSIVE; THE ADAPTATION FITS THE TRADITIONAL MELODY.)

ONCE WE WERE SLAVES

Once we were (male) slaves,
now we are free!

Once we were (female) slaves,
now we are free!

Once we were enslaved,
now we are free!

שְׁפָחוֹת וַעֲבָדִים הָיִינוּ

עֲבָדִים הָיִינוּ, הָיִינוּ.
עַתָּה בְּנֵי חוֹרִין, בְּנֵי חוֹרִין.

SH'FAḤOT VA'AVADIM
HAYÍNU

שְׁפָחוֹת הָיִינוּ.
עַתָּה בְּנוֹת, בְּנוֹת חוֹרִין.

בְּעַבְדוּת הָיִינוּ.
עַתָּה עַתָּה בְּנוֹת חוֹרִין, בְּנוֹת חוֹרִין.
עַתָּה עַתָּה בְּנֵי חוֹרִין, בְּנֵי חוֹרִין.

Avadim hayínu, hayínu.
Atah b'ney ḥorin, b'ney ḥorin.

Sh'faḥot hayínu.
Atah b'not, b'not ḥorin.

B'avdut hayínu.
Atah atah b'not ḥorin, b'not ḥorin.
Atah atah b'ney ḥorin, b'ney ḥorin.

הא לחמא עניא

THIS IS THE BREAD OF AFFLICTION

HA LAḤMA ANYA

Ha Laḥma Anya was written in Aramaic, the vernacular spoken during the Second Temple period and throughout rabbinic times.

Recalling our lives as slaves in Egypt—and, indeed, as slaves of the Nazis a mere generation ago—the words of *Ha Laḥma Anya* also call to mind the plight of those in need today: "Let all who are hungry come and eat. Let all who are in need share our Pesach."

It has become customary to invite family and friends to the seder, along with acquaintances who do not have a seder to attend. If we were also to invite strangers in our midst—refugees, exiles, those without a home—we would place ourselves in a millennia-long tradition: our forefather Abraham welcomed strangers to his tent and, with the help of his wife, Sarah, and a servant, waited on them and gave them food and water (Genesis 18:1–8).

Opening the door, as we do metaphorically when we recite *Ha Laḥma Anya*, makes porous the border between inner and outer—between our lives and the lives of others, between our selves and the greater whole of being. We open the door, and we open our hearts, fulfilling the commandment to empathize with those who are strangers to us: "You shall not oppress a stranger, for you know the feelings of a stranger, having yourselves been strangers in the land of Egypt" (Exodus 23:9).

THE LEADER LIFTS THE COVER FROM THE MATZAH AND HOLDS THE
MATZAH UP. WE SING THE TRADITIONAL ARAMAIC VERSES AND RECITE
THE ENGLISH TRANSLATION. (A FEW WORDS HAVE BEEN ADDED TO THE
ARAMAIC TO MAKE THE PASSAGE MORE GENDER-INCLUSIVE. WITH A
LITTLE MUSICAL WIGGLING, THE ADAPTATION CAN BE SUNG TO THE
TRADITIONAL MELODY.)

THIS IS THE BREAD OF AFFLICTION

You shall eat unleavened bread,
the bread of affliction,
for you departed the land of Egypt in haste.

DEUTERONOMY 16:3

If there is a needy person among you . . .
open your hand and give.

DEUTERONOMY 15:7–8

This is the bread of affliction,
which our ancestors ate
in the land of Egypt.

Let all who are hungry come and eat.
Let all who are in need
share our Pesach.

This year—here.
Next year—in a just and peaceful Israel.

This year—enslaved.
Next year—free.

HA LAḤMA ANYA

הָא לַחְמָא עַנְיָא

Tokhal-alav matzot léḥem óni
ki v'ḥipazon
yatzáta me'éretz mitzráyim.

תֹּאכַל־עָלָיו מַצּוֹת לֶחֶם עֹנִי
כִּי בְחִפָּזוֹן
יָצָאתָ מֵאֶרֶץ מִצְרָיִם.

DEUTERONOMY 16:3

דברים טז:ג

Ki-yihyeh v'kha evyon
me'aḥad aḥékha . . .
Ki-fató'aḥ tiftaḥ et-yad'kha lo.

כִּי־יִהְיֶה בְךָ אֶבְיוֹן
מֵאַחַד אַחֶיךָ . . .
כִּי־פָתֹחַ תִּפְתַּח אֶת־יָדְךָ לוֹ.

DEUTERONOMY 15:7–8

דברים טו, ז–ח

Ha laḥma,
ha laḥma anya

הָא לַחְמָא,
הָא לַחְמָא עַנְיָא

di akhálu
imhaténa v'avhaténa

דִּי אֲכָלוּ
אִמְהָתָנָא וְאַבְהָתָנָא

b'ar'a, b'ar'a d'mitzráyim,
b'ar'a, b'ar'a d'mitzráyim.

בְּאַרְעָא, בְּאַרְעָא דְמִצְרָיִם,
בְּאַרְעָא, בְּאַרְעָא דְמִצְרָיִם.

Kol dikhfin yeytey v'yeykhul,
kol ditzrikh yeytey v'yifsaḥ.

כָּל דִּכְפִין יֵיתֵי וְיֵכֻל,
כָּל דִּצְרִיךְ יֵיתֵי וְיִפְסַח.

Hashata hakha,
l'shanah habá'ah
b'ar'a d'yisra'el.

הָשַׁתָּא הָכָא,
לְשָׁנָה הַבָּאָה
בְּאַרְעָא דְיִשְׂרָאֵל.

Hashata avdey v'amhan,
l'shanah habá'ah
b'not uvney ḥorin.

הָשַׁתָּא עַבְדֵי וְאַמְהָן,
לְשָׁנָה הַבָּאָה
בְּנוֹת וּבְנֵי חוֹרִין.

OPEN DOOR
KAVANAH

A home that is open to all: the sacred promise of the United States.

No one has expressed this more eloquently than the Jewish-American poet Emma Lazarus (1849–1887). As well as being a poet, writer, and translator, Lazarus, who came from an affluent Sefardic family, devoted herself to the welfare of the poor and the Jewish immigrant community fleeing Russian pogroms.

Lazarus's poem "The New Colossus" is particularly appropriate for Pesach. In it, she joins together concern for the exiled and homeless with the yearning for freedom—twin themes of the Exodus story. And, strikingly, the contrast she draws between the "brazen giant of Greek fame" and the "Mother of Exiles" echoes the contrast between Pharaoh and the women of the Exodus story, as will be made vividly apparent when we read "Maggid: The Telling."

THE NEW COLOSSUS

Not like the brazen giant of Greek fame,
With conquering limbs astride from land to land,
Here at our sea-washed, sunset gates shall stand
A mighty woman with a torch, whose flame
Is the imprisoned lightning, and her name
Mother of Exiles. From her beacon-hand
Glows world-wide welcome; her mild eyes command
The air-bridged harbor that twin cities frame.
"Keep ancient lands, your storied pomp!" cries she
With silent lips. "Give me your tired, your poor,
Your huddled masses yearning to breathe free,
The wretched refuse of your teeming shore.
Send these, the homeless, tempest-tost to me,
I lift my lamp beside the golden door!"

WRITTEN IN 1883; AFFIXED TO THE STATUE OF LIBERTY
IN 1903

May we commit to bringing this promise to fulfillment in our time.

FREEDOM AND THE LIVES OF OTHERS
KAVANAH

In contrast to "Once We Were Slaves," in which we proclaim that we are now free, the last stanza of "This Is the Bread of Affliction" states that we are not yet free. We might consider the opposing perspectives of these passages. Recognizing that freedom is not an absolute, we might ask to what extent, and in what ways, we are free—and in what ways we are still constricted, confined, constrained. The tension between the freedom we have and the freedom we still lack suffuses the Pesach holiday.

There is an even greater contrast between the freedoms available to some of us living as citizens in the developed world and the freedoms that are available, or denied, to so many others. How many in the world are suffering enslavement, oppression, dehumanization? How many know hunger, poverty, homelessness? How many are being wounded by the vestiges and after-effects of these evils?

How much of this pain are we awake to? What are we doing to end and to repair the damage?

How much does our freedom depend on the lives of others, who may not share in our good fortune?

In his historic speech "I Have a Dream," delivered at the 1963 March on Washington for Jobs and Freedom, Dr. Martin Luther King Jr. quoted the prophet Amos (5:24) when he proclaimed: "No, no, we are not satisfied until 'justice rolls down like waters and righteousness like a mighty stream.'"

May we commit to realizing, in our own time, the dream of Martin Luther King Jr.

בכל דור ודור

IN EVERY GENERATION

B'KHOL DOR VADOR

We are about to tell the story of our flight from Egypt. As we consider its meanings, we take up the rabbis' injunction that we place ourselves inside the story, reading it as though each of us was personally liberated from slavery.

To deepen our understanding, we might project ourselves into other characters in the narrative, looking inside ourselves for Pharaoh, who controls and dominates; Moshe, who seeks confidence and calling; Miriam and the other women, who embody empathy, compassion, and connection. In addition to enriching our reading of the story, this contemplation may reveal to us parts of ourselves that we are unaware of or that we do not always wish to acknowledge—the hidden pieces of our lives, the *afikoman*s that need to be uncovered in order for us to be whole and truly free.

WE SING THESE HEBREW WORDS. THE FIRST STANZA IS A GENDER-INCLUSIVE ADAPTATION OF THE TRADITIONAL *B'KHOL DOR VADOR*. THE SECOND STANZA IS ANOTHER VARIATION, WITH A MORE PERSONAL FOCUS. BOTH STANZAS CAN BE SUNG TO THE TRADITIONAL MELODY.

IN EVERY GENERATION

In every generation,
one must see oneself
as having gone out of Egypt.

On every seder night,
with each new Telling—
a new chance to see myself
becoming free.

בְּכָל דּוֹר וָדּוֹר

בְּכָל דּוֹר וָדּוֹר
חוֹבָה עָלֵינוּ לִרְאוֹת
לִרְאוֹת אֶת עַצְמֵנוּ כְּאִלּוּ
כְּאִלּוּ יָצָאנוּ מִמִּצְרָיִם.

בְּכָל לֵיל סֵדֶר
חוֹבָה עָלַי לִרְאוֹת
לִרְאוֹת אֶת עַצְמִי כְּאִלּוּ
כְּאִלּוּ יָצָאתִי מִמִּצְרָיִם.

B'KHOL DOR VADOR

B'khol dor vador
ḥovah aléynu lir'ot
lir'ot et atzménu k'ilu
k'ilu yatzánu mimitzráyim.

B'khol leyl séder
ḥovah alay lir'ot
lir'ot et atzmi k'ilu
k'ilu yatzáti mimitzráyim.

73

לקראת המגיד

TELLING ONESELF INTO THE STORY

The portal is open;
you step into a foreign place.

The first face you meet
is your own.

Approaching from the distance—
a procession.

Do you join?

Do you join, knowing
where the path will take you?

Do you join,
not knowing?

The story is yours
to make your own.

Do you come along?

מגיד

MAGGID: THE TELLING

PRESENTATION OF THE TEXT

The word *haggadah* means "telling," and a *maggid* is, literally, the one who tells the story. Tonight we take turns being the *maggid*. We tell the story of our liberation from Egypt as it appears in the Book of Exodus, condensed here and presented in six parts.

Within the story, indented, are quotations from the Bible and from the Midrash (rabbinic commentaries).

New commentaries by the author of this haggadah are interspersed throughout the story. They appear, unindented, in bold type.

If necessary to save time, the story can be read without the indented biblical and midrashic passages or the new commentaries. However, reading the Maggid in its entirety will provide more food for thought and discussion.

For those who wish an even shorter seder, "Maggid: The Telling, Abbreviated" may be found at the end of the full Maggid. After reading the abbreviated version, participants might choose to read and discuss the commentaries to selected passages in the full version.

OVERVIEW AND THEMES

The Maggid is the centerpiece of the haggadah. The story it tells of our liberation from slavery is also the story of our emergence into peoplehood. We focus tonight on the first fifteen chapters of the Book of Exodus, beginning with the Israelites' enslavement in Egypt and climaxing with the parting of the Sea of Reeds. But the biblical story of our becoming a people does not end with the crossing of the sea; it continues through the Book of Exodus and beyond. The journey from Egypt that we begin to tell tonight will ultimately culminate in a return home—to the Promised Land of Canaan.

In this sense, the Exodus story is also a birth story, a story of beginnings. It is one of the two foundational narratives of Jewish civilization, the other being the Creation story in Genesis 1–3. We can think of the creation of the world *and* our liberation from Egypt as the great creation myths of our people. To say that we read these narratives as myths is not to say that they are untrue; myths are true not because they are factually or historically accurate but because they say something powerfully true about our common humanity and, in the case of the Exodus, about who we are as a people.

We read the Exodus story closely, as literature, without attempting to rewrite or "update" it, seeking, rather, to understand what it represented in the time of its composition and inquiring what meaning it has for us now. We do not alter the "God-language" of the narrative, as this would profoundly distort its original meaning: in these chapters of the Book of Exodus, God is unequivocally male.

The Exodus story is also about concealments and revealments. As we tell it tonight, we will notice a recurrent motif of hiding: individuals' hiding from others, their hiding from themselves, and their being partially hidden from the reader by being unnamed.

We will also see the openings-up of that which is concealed, exemplified especially by Moshe's increasing awareness of his Hebrew identity and his gradual awakening to his purpose and calling as a prophet. Moshe's story begins in a hidden place among the river reeds. It ends with Moshe and the Israelites singing the triumphant "Song of the Sea" in an opened-up expanse of land.

ONE
ENSLAVEMENT IN EGYPT

EXODUS 1:8–14

The Book of Exodus begins in Egypt, where the Israelites have been living, after Joseph, his brothers, and the Pharaoh he once served have all died. Feeling threatened by the Israelites, who have increased greatly in number, the new Pharaoh embarks on a campaign to subdue them, forcing them into slavery.

> Pharaoh said to his people, "Look, the Israelite people are much too numerous for us. Let us deal shrewdly with them so that they may not increase" . . . So they set taskmasters over them to oppress them with forced labor . . . Ruthlessly they made life bitter for them with harsh labor at mortar and bricks, and with all sorts of tasks in the field.

TWO
MIRIAM AND THE WOMEN

EXODUS 1:15–22

Pharaoh commands the Hebrew midwives Shifrah and Pu'ah to kill all newborn Israelite males after they are delivered. The midwives, fearing God, let the boys live. Pharaoh summons the midwives and demands they explain their disobedience; they reply with an ingenious lie.

> Pharaoh said to them, "Why have you done this thing, letting the boys live?" The midwives said to Pharaoh, "Because the Hebrew women are not like the Egyptian women: they are vigorous. Before the midwife can come to them, they have given birth."

God deals well with the midwives. The people multiply and increase greatly.

Pharaoh, who does not fear the Israelite God, charges his people to throw every Hebrew newborn boy into the Nile but to let every girl live.

The story emphasizes the importance of the midwives, mentioning them multiple times; they are the only women who are given names in this early part of the narrative. They are referred to as Hebrew midwives, but it is unclear whether they are themselves Hebrews or whether they are Egyptians who are midwives for the Israelite women. In either case, their action is not only compassionate but daring. If they are indeed Egyptians, their defiance of their king in order to save children who are not of their own people is truly extraordinary.

EXODUS 2:1–10

A baby boy—who will turn out to be Moshe—is born to an Israelite couple. When the baby's mother sees how good (*tov*) he is, she hides him for three months. When she can hide him no longer, she puts the child into a *tevah*—usually translated as "basket"—and places the *tevah* among the reeds by the banks of the Nile. His sister—who is not named at this point but who will, thirteen chapters later, be called Miriam—stations herself at a distance, to learn what may befall him.

There is a sly bit of irony here: Moshe's mother indeed places her son in the Nile—but encased and hidden in a protective little boat. (The word *tevah* appears only twice in the Bible: here and in the story of Noah, where it refers to an ark. In both instances the *tevah* functions to preserve life.) The Creation myth in Genesis is also echoed here: Moshe's mother calls him *tov* (good) just as God proclaims that His creations are *tov*.

The motif of hiding is introduced here. As Miriam watches over her baby brother concealed in the reeds, she must also hide herself. Because she is nameless, we might say that she is doubly "hidden"—first from the Egyptians, and then, partly, from us. Miriam's mother, the first to hide Moshe, is also nameless, and so we might say that she too is partially hidden.

Spying the basket, Pharaoh's daughter recognizes that the baby inside must be a Hebrew child, and she takes pity on him. Miriam (acting as ingeniously as the midwives) comes forward and offers to find a nursemaid. When Pharaoh's daughter accepts the offer, Miriam fetches her mother—who is, of course, also the baby's mother. Pharaoh's daughter pays Moshe's mother to nurse him and later takes him in as her son. She names him Moshe, explaining, "I drew him out of the water."

In acting to save the baby's life, Pharaoh's daughter is unique in the Bible: she takes in a child who is not of her people and raises him as her own. Hers is an act of great compassion that also constitutes a rebellion against authority: in saving the Hebrew child she defies the orders of her father, who is both king and god to the Egyptians.

Despite her remarkable action, Pharaoh's daughter's name is also withheld from us and—unlike Miriam, who will be called by name at the apex of the story—she remains nameless to the end. Indeed, we will not hear any more about Pharaoh's daughter in the Book of Exodus, despite the large part we might assume an adoptive mother would have played in the development of Moshe's character.

As we have seen, the empathetic acts of all the women in the story exemplify an ethic of care. While the biblical narrative focuses on the male characters, the fate of the Hebrews is equally dependent on the less-elaborated acts of the women. As Rabbi Avira expounded: "Israel was redeemed from Egypt on account of the righteous women of that generation" (b. Talmud Sotah 116; Exodus Rabbah 1:12).

THREE
MOSHE'S CALLING

Moshe is mentioned only once in the traditional haggadah; there, the rabbis give God all the credit for our liberation. Yet Moshe is at the center of the biblical narrative, which traces his development from infancy to full adulthood.

It is a stunning fact that none of the women in the Exodus story are mentioned at all in the haggadah. Tonight, when we finish reading the Maggid, as we say a blessing over Miriam's Cup, we will call to mind all the women of the story.

EXODUS 2:11–14
Moshe grows up and sees the misery of the Hebrews, "his brothers." He observes an Egyptian beating a Hebrew and kills the Egyptian, hiding him in the sand.

This is the first moment in which Moshe is shown to be aware that the Hebrews are his kin—a pivotal point in his personal development. His act of hiding the Egyptian coincides with the beginning of his emergence from "self-hiding"—that is, his coming to awareness that although he was raised as an Egyptian, he also belongs to another people. That awareness will ultimately lead him to find his calling.

The next day, Moshe sees two Hebrews fighting. He intercedes, asking the aggressor why he is striking his "fellow." The aggressor retorts, "Are you going to kill me the way you killed the Egyptian?" Moshe now realizes that the matter is known: he can no longer hide who he is and what he has done.

EXODUS 2:15–22

In retribution for Moshe's slaying of the Egyptian, Pharaoh seeks to kill Moshe, who flees to the land of Midian, near Mount Horeb (Mount Sinai), and sits beside a well. The seven daughters of Yitro, a priest in Midian, come to water their flock, but shepherds drive them off. Moshe defends the women, who believe he is an Egyptian and invite him into their father's household. Moshe stays, marrying one of the daughters, Tziporah. She gives birth to a son, whom Moshe names Gershom (literally, "a stranger there"), saying, "I have been a stranger in a strange land."

The story suggests that Moshe had two mothers and belonged to two peoples, the Israelites and the Egyptians. We might wonder then why Moshe feels himself to have been a stranger in Egypt, given that he was raised as a member of the royal family. Is this an indication of his increasing alienation from his Egyptian roots and of his growing self-identity as a Hebrew?

We have seen three events revealing Moshe's character, and, specifically, the keen sense of justice that propels his actions. Killing a brutal Egyptian taskmaster, Moshe defends a Hebrew slave. Interceding in a fight between two Hebrews, Moshe acts as a mediator. And in standing up for Yitro's daughters, he protects the weak. God chooses Moshe to be His prophet only after Moshe has proven himself worthy of the tasks before him.

EXODUS 2:23–25
Pharaoh dies, the Israelites continue to suffer, and God hears them and remembers His covenant.

EXODUS 3:1–20
Moshe goes to Horeb (Sinai) where he witnesses a miraculous sight.

> An angel of God appeared to him in a blazing fire out of a bush—*s'neh bo'er*. . . . Moshe said, "I must turn and see this marvelous sight; why doesn't the bush burn up?" [Then] God called to him out of the bush: "Moshe! Moshe!" He answered, *"Hinéni* (Here I am)." And He said, "Do not come closer . . . the place on which you stand is holy ground. I am," He said, "the God of your fathers, God of Abraham, God of Isaac, and God of Jacob." And Moshe hid his face, for he was afraid to look at God.

This moment foreshadows the giving of the Torah and the Ten Commandments on Mount Sinai. At the burning bush, God announces Himself as the God of Moshe's forefathers. At Sinai, God again announces Himself: "I יְהֹוָה am your God who brought you out of the land of Egypt, the house of bondage: you shall have no other gods besides Me." (יְהֹוָה is the ineffable name of the Divinity, often represented in English as YHWH.) A *midrash* points out the word play between *s'neh* (bush) and *sinai* (Sinai).

We find in this passage another kind of hiding: at the moment that God reveals Himself to Moshe out of the burning bush, Moshe shields his eyes, preventing himself from beholding the awesome power before him, lest he be overcome by the sight. This is a special form of hiding, born of fear and awe.

God tells Moshe that He is mindful of the sufferings of His people and, with Moshe as His emissary, He will rescue them and bring them to Canaan, "a good and spacious land, a land flowing with milk and honey." He tells Moshe to go to the new Pharaoh and free God's people. This is the beginning of an impassioned dialogue between God and Moshe, in which Moshe repeatedly tries to convince God that he is not the right person for this task:

> "Who am I that I should go to Pharaoh and free the Israelites from Egypt?" And He said, "I will be with you." . . . Moshe said to God, "When I come to the Israelites and say to them, 'The God of your fathers has sent me to you,' and they ask me, 'What is His name?' what shall I say to them?" And God said to Moshe, "*Ehyeh-Asher-Ehyeh* (I Am That I Am) . . . Yet I know that the king of Egypt will let you go only because of a greater might. So I will . . . smite Egypt with various wonders that I will work upon them."

EXODUS 4:1–17

Moshe protests further: "What if [the people] do not believe me?" God tells Moshe that He will empower him to perform miracles to persuade the doubters. And if the people still don't believe that God has appeared to Moshe, He will empower Moshe to turn the Nile water into blood—the first of ten plagues that God will visit upon the Egyptians.

Moshe continues to plead with God: "Please, O God, I have never been a man of words . . . I am slow of speech and heavy of tongue." God presents Moshe with a staff for performing miracles and appoints his brother, Aaron, to be his spokesman.

FOUR
MOSHE, GOD, AND PHARAOH—CONFRONTATIONS

EXODUS 4:18–23
Moshe goes back to Egypt with his wife and sons to undertake the task appointed him by God to free the people.

> And God said to Moshe, "Perform before Pharaoh all the marvels that I have put within your power. I, however, will harden his heart so that he will not let the people go."

We might ask why God does not simply strike Pharaoh down and free God's people. Such action would not only spare the Egyptians the plagues but would immediately end, rather than prolong, the suffering of the Israelites. This seems an especially cruel choice on God's part. In subsequent chapters, God will reveal His explicit purpose.

EXODUS 5:1–23
Moshe and Aaron go to Pharaoh to demand that he let the people go. Pharaoh refuses and imposes even harsher conditions on the Israelites: in addition to making bricks, they must now gather straw for the bricks. Moshe turns to God:

"Why did You bring harm upon this people? Ever since I came to Pharaoh to speak in Your name, he has dealt more harshly with this people. And You did not save Your people."

Moshe is no longer pleading; he is challenging God. He has already established himself as a leader; at this moment, interceding with God on behalf of the people, he becomes a prophet.

Later, in the wilderness, when God seeks to destroy the Israelites in retribution for their sinning (their creating the Golden Calf and sending scouts into Canaan), we will see Moshe pleading to save the people's lives. Moshe the Prophet brings human compassion to bear, trying to bend God's impulses toward mercy.

EXODUS 6:2–7:13

God tells Moshe that He will redeem the Israelites "with an outstretched arm and through extraordinary chastisements." Once more, Moshe resists his assignment, but God insists, repeating His intention to "toughen Pharaoh's heart." Pharaoh will let the people go because God will display a "greater might."

Here we find God's answer to the question that we posed earlier: *Why does He harden Pharaoh's heart?* As He states here and will reiterate multiple times, He does so in order to display His powers. He will harden Pharaoh's heart after each of ten plagues that He will visit upon the Egyptians.

We now have more fully drawn portraits of the three male protagonists. God is both prideful and an upholder of justice. He acts not only to punish the Egyptians but to demonstrate that He is the greatest of all gods.

Pharaoh is a one-dimensional figure with no redeeming character-istics. He is an authoritarian dictator and xenophobic oppressor.

The character of Moshe is more complex than that of either God or Pharaoh, and in many ways the story belongs to him. He is a modest, self-effacing man who reluctantly develops over the course of the narrative into a great leader and prophet. An empathetic advocate for his people, he is also capable of anger and even violence.

EXODUS 7:14–11:7

These are the first nine plagues:

First plague—*dam* (turning the Nile river into blood); second plague—*tz'fardé'a* (unleashing multitudes of frogs); third plague—*kinim* (unleashing lice); fourth plague—*arov* (releasing swarms of insects); fifth plague—*déver* (striking the cattle with disease); sixth plague—*sh'ḥin* (causing boils to erupt on people and animals); seventh plague—*barad* (causing hail to fall); eighth plague—*arbeh* (releasing locusts); ninth plague—*ḥóshekh* (submerging Egypt in thick darkness).

God tells Moshe and Aaron that He will bring one more plague upon Egypt: He will kill all first-born Egyptians and their first-born animals. Then Pharaoh will let God's people go.

EXODUS 12:1–13:16

Before God imposes the last, most terrible, plague, He instructs the Israelites to sacrifice lambs and to smear the blood on the lintels of the Israelite houses. When "the Slaughterer" comes to take the Egyptians' first-borns, he will "pass over" (*pasaḥ*) the Israelites' homes. (The word *pasaḥ* is the root of the name of the festival of *pésaḥ*.) God instructs Moshe how to make the Pesach festival honoring Him: in remembrance of God's freeing them from Egypt, the Israelites are to dedicate their firstborns to God and to celebrate for seven days, during which they shall eat only matzah.

EXODUS 12:29–34

Tenth plague—*makat b'khorot* (slaying of the first-born): in the middle of the night, God slays the first-born of the Egyptians and the first-born of their animals. Pharaoh at last tells Moshe to take his people and go. The Egyptians, fearing death, urge the Israelites to leave. The Israelites take their unleavened dough and hasten to the wilderness.

The last two plagues—darkness and the slaying of the first-born— echo the Genesis Creation story: the separation of light and darkness on the first day of creation, and the infliction of mortality on humanity as a result of the sins of Adam and Eve.

WE PAUSE TO CHANT THE NAMES OF THE TEN PLAGUES. WITH EACH PLAGUE, WE DIMINISH BY A DROP THE WINE IN OUR CUPS, TO EXPRESS OUR EMPATHY FOR THE SUFFERING OF THE EGYPTIANS.

THE TEN PLAGUES

עֶשֶׂר הַמַּכּוֹת

dam (blood)   דָּם

tz'fardé'a (frogs)   צְפַרְדֵּעַ

kinim (lice)   כִּנִּים

arov (insects)   עָרֹב

déver (cattle disease)   דֶּבֶר

sh'ḥin (boils)   שְׁחִין

barad (hail)   בָּרָד

arbeh (locusts)   אַרְבֶּה

ḥóshekh (darkness)   חֹשֶׁךְ

makat b'khorot (slaying of the first-born)   מַכַּת בְּכוֹרוֹת

WE RETURN TO THE STORY.

FIVE
EXODUS FROM EGYPT

EXODUS 13:21–22

God appears as a pillar of cloud by day and a pillar of fire at night so that the Israelites can follow Him through the desert to the Sea of Reeds.

EXODUS 14:4–30

Once again God hardens Pharaoh's heart, so that Pharaoh will change his mind about letting the Israelites leave Egypt. God declares He will gain glory by destroying Pharaoh and the Egyptian army.

The Egyptians chase the Israelites. The Israelites are frightened; they cry out to God and Moshe, saying they would be better off remaining slaves in Egypt:

> "Was it for want of graves in Egypt that you brought us to die in the wilderness? What have you done to us, taking us out of Egypt?"

This is the first of many instances in which the Israelites complain to Moshe about their privations in the wilderness, pleading to return to the comforts they claim to have had in Egypt. Their reaction calls to mind an adolescent's ambivalence toward freedom: the desire to break through restrictions and go out on one's own, combined with the fear of leaving the only home one knows. We might see the Israelites' behavior as an intermediary stage in their maturation as a people.

Moshe reassures the Israelites; he stretches out his arm, as God directs, and parts the Sea of Reeds, allowing the Israelites to cross.

In parting the sea at this climactic moment, God, through Moshe, opens a space for the Israelites to pass through—what might be viewed as a birth passage for the nation. This birth recalls another great birthing, part of the Creation story told in Genesis 1:6–7, in which God makes "an expanse in the midst of the water that it may separate water from water."

The association of the Exodus story with the story of the world's creation—the two foundational events of Judaism—is referred to in every *kiddush* blessing, every sanctification over wine for holidays and the Sabbath, which we still say today. Psalm 136 also

makes a connection between the Creation and the Exodus, reciting the stages of creation followed by the stages of the Israelites' liberation from Egypt.

The parting of the Sea of Reeds also prefigures the moment when, in Joshua 3:13–17, the Israelites cross through the parted waters of the Jordan into the Promised Land. Psalm 114, part of which we sing tonight in *Hallel*, connects these two miraculous events, which provide a framework for our becoming a people. The parting of the Sea of Reeds is the first step in our journey to reach the Promised Land; with the parting of the Jordan at the end of the journey, we enter the land.

God's opening-up of the sea might also be viewed as a reversal of the scene at the near-beginning of the narrative, in which Moshe's mother encloses the baby in a little boat and hides him in the sheltering confinement of the reeds.

The Egyptians follow; Moshe stretches out his arm again. The waters close up, God hurls the Egyptians into the sea, and they drown.

These acts are another ironic reversal, a retribution for Pharaoh's earlier attempt to cast the Hebrew babies into the Nile. The circle of the narrative is beginning to close.

The rabbis express ambivalence toward this portion of the story, as we may do as well:

> When the Holy One was about to drown the Egyptians in the sea, Uzza, heavenly prince of Egypt, rose up and prostrated himself before the Holy One, saying: "Master of the

universe, You created the world by the measure of mercy. Why then do You wish to drown my children?"

The Holy One gathered the entire heavenly household and said to them: "You be the judge." At that, the heavenly princes of the other nations began to speak up on behalf of Egypt.

[Then the angels Michael and Gabriel brought evidence of the cruelty of the Egyptians, saying to God:] "Thus did the Egyptians enslave Your children." Whereupon the Holy One sat in judgment over the Egyptians in accord with the measure of justice and drowned them in the sea.

In that instant, the ministering angels wished to utter a song before the Holy One, but He rebuked them, saying, "The works of My hands are drowning in the sea, and you would utter a song in My presence!" (b. Talmud *Sanhedrin* 39b)

In this passage the rabbis raise challenging ethical questions: What is the proper balance between compassion and justice? Does the struggle against oppression allow, or at times even necessitate, the use of violence and the infliction of suffering on others?

EXODUS 15:1–19
Moshe and the Israelites sing the "Song of the Sea," praising God for rescuing them and slaying the Egyptians:

I will sing to God
for He has triumphed gloriously.
Horse and driver
He has hurled into the sea.
. . . .
Pharaoh's chariots and his army
He has cast into the sea,
and the best of his officers
drowned in the Sea of Reeds.
The deeps covered them,
they descended into the depths like a stone.
. . . .
You sent forth your fury, God;
it consumed them like straw.
At the breath of Your nostrils
the waters piled up,
the running waters stood up like a wall,
the deeps froze in the heart of the sea.
. . . .
You made Your wind blow;
the sea covered them.
They sank like lead
in the majestic waters.

Who is like You, O God,
among the celestials?
Who is like You, majestic in holiness,
awesome in splendor, working wonders!

SIX

MIRIAM THE PROPHETESS

EXODUS 15: 20–21

Miriam and the women celebrate.

> Then Miriam the Prophetess, Aaron's sister, took a timbrel
> in her hand, and all the women went out after her, dancing
> with timbrels. And Miriam chanted for them: "Sing to God
> for He has triumphed gloriously. Horse and driver He has
> hurled into the sea."

**The Pesach story has come full circle. The sister of Moshe and
Aaron has been given a name—not just a name but an appella-
tion: Miriam the Prophetess. She has emerged from a half-hid-
den place into prominence, much as the Israelites have emerged
from confinement into freedom and promise. At the story's
apex, the moment of the Israelites' triumph, she is at the center of a community of women celebrants. She takes the lead;
she has earned it.**

**And yet, in contrast to what we have been told of Moshe's birth,
maturation, and ultimate evolution into the status of leader
and prophet, we have heard almost nothing of Miriam's biog-
raphy. Given this omission, it is not apparent why the Bible refers to Miriam as a prophetess, especially considering that she
does not perform the prophet's characteristic tasks of warning,
predicting, and interceding with God on behalf of the people.
The rabbis account for this by inventing stories of their own, in
which Miriam indeed prophesies. We might propose that Miriam deserves her recognition as a prophetess not because of her**

words but because of her actions to save Moshe, who will become the savior of the Israelites, making Miriam the guarantor of the people's future.

In another *midrash*, the rabbis associate Miriam with a well—rightly so, as she is a life-source for the ancient Hebrews, a "sustainer," as the Talmud puts it:

> Rabbi Yossei, son of Rabbi Yehudah said: "Three great sustainers arose for the people of Israel during the Exodus from Egypt: Moshe, Aaron, and Miriam. And three good gifts were given by means of them: the well of water [which gave the Israelites water in the wilderness], a pillar of cloud [by means of which God led the Israelites out of Egypt by day], and the manna [the food provided by God in the wilderness]. The well was in the merit of Miriam." (b. Talmud *Ta'anit* 9a)

MAGGID: THE TELLING, ABBREVIATED
(EXODUS 1:1–15:20)

The Book of Exodus begins in Egypt, where the Israelites have been living, after Joseph, his brothers, and the Pharaoh he once served have all died. The new Pharaoh—feeling threatened by the Israelites, who have increased greatly in number—embarks on a campaign to subdue them, forcing them into slavery. Eventually, Pharaoh decrees that all Hebrew boys must be killed at birth.

Two Hebrew midwives, Shifrah and Pu'ah, resist the decree by claiming Hebrew women are so vigorous that they give birth before the midwives can come to them.

A Hebrew mother saves her newborn son by placing him in a wicker basket and hiding him amid reeds in the Nile. The baby's sister watches over him from a distance. Pharaoh's daughter discovers the baby. The baby's sister—who goes unnamed here but later will be identified as Miriam—comes forward, asking the princess if she would like the baby to be nursed by a Hebrew woman. Pharaoh's daughter assents, and Miriam returns the infant to his own mother. Later, he is taken to the princess, who adopts him as her own and names him Moshe.

Moshe grows up and becomes aware of his Hebrew origins. One day he kills an Egyptian who is beating an Israelite slave. In retribution, Pharaoh seeks to kill Moshe, who flees to Midian in the Sinai and sits down beside a well. The seven daughters of Yitro, a priest in Midian, come to the well to water their flock, but shepherds drive them off. Moshe defends the women, who invite him into their father's household. Moshe stays, marrying one of the daughters, Tziporah. She gives birth to a son, whom Moshe names Gershom (literally, "a stranger there"), saying, "I have been a stranger in a strange land."

Concerned for the suffering of the Israelites, God appears to Moshe from a bush that is burning but is not consumed and relays His plan to send Moshe back to Egypt to lead the Israelites to Canaan, "a land flowing with milk and honey." Moshe resists, citing his slowness of speech, but God presents him with a staff for performing miracles and instructs him to take his brother, Aaron, along as his spokesperson. When Moshe asks God's name, so that he may tell the Hebrews who is saving them, God replies, "*Ehyeh-Asher-Ehyeh* (I Am That I Am)."

Moshe and Aaron return to Egypt, where they confront Pharaoh, demanding he release the Hebrews; but God purposely hardens Pharaoh's heart so that he will not relent. Pharaoh increases the workload of the Israelites. God responds to Pharaoh's stubbornness by inflicting a series of ten plagues on Egypt; before each plague, Moshe demands the Israelites' release. After each plague, God hardens Pharaoh's heart so that he will refuse the demands, the better for God to display His powers. Before the tenth plague, the killing of the firstborn Egyptians, Moshe instructs the Israelites to mark their doorposts with the blood of a sacrificed lamb, as a sign for "the Slaughterer" to pass over their homes and spare them.

God enjoins the Israelites to commemorate this day forever by dedicating their firstborn children to God and by celebrating the festival of Pesach for seven days. He commands them to eat only matzah, unleavened bread, during the festival.

WE PAUSE TO CHANT THE NAMES OF THE TEN PLAGUES. WITH EACH PLAGUE, WE DIMINISH BY A DROP THE WINE IN OUR CUPS, TO EXPRESS OUR EMPATHY FOR THE SUFFERING OF THE EGYPTIANS.

THE TEN PLAGUES עֶשֶׂר הַמַּכּוֹת

dam (blood) דָּם

tz'fardé'a (frogs) צְפַרְדֵּעַ

kinim (lice) כִּנִּים

arov (insects) עָרֹב

déver (cattle disease) דֶּבֶר

sh'hin (boils) שְׁחִין

barad (hail) בָּרָד

arbeh (locusts) אַרְבֶּה

hóshekh (darkness) חֹשֶׁךְ

makat b'khorot (slaying of the first-born) מַכַּת בְּכוֹרוֹת

WE RETURN TO THE STORY.

Finally, Pharaoh relents, releasing the Israelites.

Guided by a pillar of cloud in daylight and a pillar of fire at night, Moshe and the Israelites walk toward the Sea of Reeds. Pharaoh, having changed his mind one last time about freeing the Israelites, gives chase with his warriors. The Israelites complain that Moshe is leading them to their death, but God, through Moshe, parts the sea so that the people may cross over. Moshe then closes back the waters, drowning the Egyptian army when it attempts to follow.

In response to this miracle, Moshe and the people praise God in the "Song of the Sea." Miriam—who is now named and given the title prophetess—takes a timbrel in her hand, and all the women follow her with timbrels, dancing. Miriam chants for them the opening lines of "Song of the Sea": "Sing to God, for He has triumphed gloriously. Horse and driver He has hurled into the sea."

אחרי המגיד

AFTER THE MAGGID:
CELEBRATING THE STORY

כוס מרים

MIRIAM'S CUP

KOS MIRYAM

TO HONOR MIRIAM, THE FIRST WOMAN PROPHET, AND THE OTHER HEROINES OF THE EXODUS STORY, WE LIFT OUR CUPS, FILLED WITH SPRING WATER, RECALLING MIRIAM'S WELL. WE SAY THIS BLESSING, AND DRINK.

MIRIAM'S CUP

Miriam the Prophet, sister of Aaron,
took a timbrel in her hand,
and all the women went out after her,
dancing with timbrels.

EXODUS 15:20

Zion heard and was happy,
the daughters of Judah rejoiced.

PSALM 97:8

Let us bless the living waters—
fountains and wellsprings,
rivulets, rivers, and streams—
that sustain all life.

כּוֹס מִרְיָם

וַתִּקַּח מִרְיָם הַנְּבִיאָה אֲחוֹת אַהֲרֹן
אֶת־הַתֹּף בְּיָדָהּ
וַתֵּצֶאןָ כָל־הַנָּשִׁים אַחֲרֶיהָ
בְּתֻפִּים וּבִמְחֹלֹת.

שמות טו:כ

שָׁמְעָה וַתִּשְׂמַח צִיּוֹן
וַתָּגֵלְנָה בְּנוֹת יְהוּדָה.

תהלים צז:ח

נְבָרֵךְ אֶת מֵי הָעֲיָנוֹת
וּמֵי הַנְּחָלִים
וּמֵי הַנְּהָרוֹת—
מַיִם חַיִּים
הַמַּרְוִים כָּל חָי.

KOS MIRYAM

Vatikaḥ miryam han'vi'ah aḥot aharon
et-hatof b'yadah
vatetzéna khol-hanashim aharéha
b'tupim uvimḥolot.

EXODUS 15:20

Sham'ah vatismaḥ tziyon
vatagélnah b'not y'hudah.

PSALM 97:8

N'varekh et mey ha'ayanot
umey han'ḥalim
umey han'harot—
máyim ḥayim
hamarvim kol ḥay.

107

דיינו

IT WOULD HAVE BEEN ENOUGH

DAYÉNU

A medieval entry into the haggadah, *Dayénu* is a rousing song of gratitude. The full Hebrew version contains fourteen linked verses, each acknowledging a gift from God to the Israelites during their journey from Egypt to Canaan.

WE SING THREE OF THE HEBREW VERSES TO THE FAMILIAR MELODY.

IT WOULD HAVE BEEN ENOUGH

If we had only been led out of Egypt,
it would have been enough for us!

If we had only been given Shabbat,
it would have been enough for us!

If we had only been given the Torah,
it would have been enough for us!

דַּיֵּנוּ

אִלּוּ הוֹצִי־הוֹצִיאָנוּ,
הוֹצִיאָנוּ מִמִּצְרַיִם,
הוֹצִיאָנוּ מִמִּצְרַיִם,
דַּיֵּנוּ!

DAYÉNU

Ilu hotzi-hotzi'ánu,
hotzi'ánu mimitzráyim,
hotzi'ánu mimitzráyim,
dayénu!

דַּי־דַּיֵּנוּ, דַּי־דַּיֵּנוּ,
דַּי־דַּיֵּנוּ, דַּיֵּנוּ, דַּיֵּנוּ!

Day-day-énu, day-day-énu,
day-day-énu, dayénu, dayénu!

אִלּוּ נָתַן, נָתַן לָנוּ,
נָתַן לָנוּ אֶת הַשַּׁבָּת,
נָתַן לָנוּ אֶת הַשַּׁבָּת,
דַּיֵּנוּ!

Ilu nátan, nátan lánu,
nátan lánu et hashabbat,
nátan lánu et hashabbat,
dayénu!

דַּי־דַּיֵּנוּ, דַּי־דַּיֵּנוּ,
דַּי־דַּיֵּנוּ, דַּיֵּנוּ, דַּיֵּנוּ!

Day-day-énu, day-day-énu,
day-day-énu, dayénu, dayénu!

אִלּוּ נָתַן, נָתַן לָנוּ,
נָתַן לָנוּ אֶת הַתּוֹרָה,
נָתַן לָנוּ אֶת הַתּוֹרָה,
דַּיֵּנוּ!

Ilu nátan, nátan lánu,
nátan lánu et hatorah,
nátan lánu et hatorah,
dayénu!

דַּי־דַּיֵּנוּ, דַּי־דַּיֵּנוּ,
דַּי־דַּיֵּנוּ, דַּיֵּנוּ, דַּיֵּנוּ!

Day-day-énu, day-day-énu,
day-day-énu, dayénu, dayénu!

NONETHELESS

Had you come just a few moments sooner,
you might have witnessed the molting—
the splitting of the silk
and the sudden bright emergence,
the wings filling with blood,
the last drops of moisture shaken down.
And then, the first ascents.

As it is, you find a single black butterfly,
smaller than the flat of your thumb,
its underside speckled with baneberry blood,
its topside striped with the piercing blue
of a late-June sky.

When you follow it to a slab of mossy rock
you see the whole throng of hatchlings—
one dozen, two dozen butterflies
all dipped in the same midnight ink.
All of them together
in a spot no bigger than a maple leaf—

There.
Just being there.
Enough.

WHAT IS ENOUGH?
KAVANAH

We begin as nothing, and we end as nothing. And in between—everything, and nothing. In between—joy and sorrow, beauty and decay. Everything ours to partake of, ours to bear. Ours to see, to know, to give birth to—and to let go.

None of it ours to have.

Not even our selves are ours to have. We belong to a wholeness so great we cannot even conceive of it.

No, it is not a belonging; nothing owns us. We are simply part of it. We came out of it, and we will return to it. We do not ever leave it, we are part of it forever.

And is this not enough, more than enough?

ברכת פרי הגפן

FRUIT OF THE VINE

BIRKAT P'RI HAGÉFEN

WE CONCLUDE OUR CELEBRATION OF THE MAGGID WITH THE SECOND
CUP OF WINE. WE FILL THE WINE CUPS, SAY THE BLESSING, AND DRINK.

FRUIT OF THE VINE

They will plant vineyards and drink their wine,
they will make gardens and eat their fruits.

AMOS 9:14

Let us bless the ever-flowing wellspring
that nourishes fruit on the vine.

בִּרְכַּת פְּרִי הַגֶּפֶן

וְנָטְעוּ כְרָמִים וְשָׁתוּ אֶת־יֵינָם
וְעָשׂוּ גַנּוֹת וְאָכְלוּ אֶת־פְּרִיהֶם.

עמוס ט:יד

נְבָרֵךְ אֶת הַמַּעְיָן הַשׁוֹפֵעַ
הַמַּרְוֶה אֶת פְּרִי הַגֶּפֶן.

BIRKAT P'RI HAGÉFEN

V'nat'u kh'ramim v'shatu et-yeynam
v'asu ganot v'akh'lu et-p'rihem.

AMOS 9:14

N'varekh et hama'yan hashofé'a
hamarveh et p'ri hagéfen.

115

הלל 1: תהילות חדשות

NEW POEMS OF PRAISE

HALLEL 1: T'HILOT ḤADASHOT

The word *hallel* means "praise," and *t'hilim*, the Hebrew word for the biblical Book of Psalms, derives from the same word-root. To praise is to be fully alive: "The dead cannot praise . . . nor can those who descend into silence" (Psalm 115:17).

The traditional *Hallel* section of the haggadah is a group of biblical psalms and, indeed, many are poems of praise containing vividly animated portrayals of nature. It is customary to sing the *Hallel* psalms in two places in the seder. Part 2 of our *Hallel* is found in the closing section of this haggadah; there we will sing verses excerpted from biblical psalms. In part 1, we read new poems depicting the vitality and abundance of the natural world.

SONG OF JOY

Heaven plays and the earth takes pleasure,
the sea's creatures roar with delight,
small lives of the field leap with joy.

The trees—fresh and running with sap—
lift their branches in song.
The rivers spill onto the banks,
rippling, rushing.

Together the mountains sing,
the many islands are glad,
and the world rejoices.

Break into music, let your joy sail out,
let it crash upon the rocks!
Let your gratitude rise in waves!
Make melody with harps and horns!

In old age, we will still bear fruit.

INSPIRED BY VERSES FROM PSALMS 92 AND 96–98

THE FEAST

The laden arms of the oak, the elm,
and the agitated hunger of the small jays,

the fat globes of white sugarmum
where bees suck love,

and you, in the morning shade,
tasting the new day, sharp

and alive on your tongue,
are a chorus that says,

Indulge:
The world is abundant—

this loving, dying world
to which we are given,

out of which we have come—
O body of the world,

eat with joy
the body of the world.

THE BREATH OF ALL LIFE

The breath of all life will bless,
the body will exclaim:

Were our mouths filled with song as the sea
and our tongues lapping joy like the waves

and our lips singing praises broad as the sky
and our eyes like the sun and the moon

and our arms open wide as the eagle's wings
and our feet leaping light as the deer's,

it would not be enough to tell
the wonder.

BASED ON A PRAYER THAT TRADITIONALLY
CONCLUDES *HALLEL*

NISHMAT KOL ḤAY

נִשְׁמַת כָּל חַי

Nishmat kol ḥay t'varekh	נִשְׁמַת כָּל חַי תְּבָרֵךְ
v'rú'aḥ kol basar t'fa'er:	וְרוּחַ כָּל בָּשָׂר תְּפָאֵר:
Ilu fínu maley shirah kayam	אִלּוּ פִינוּ מָלֵא שִׁירָה כַּיָּם
ulshonénu rinah kahamon galav	וּלְשׁוֹנֵנוּ רִנָּה כַּהֲמוֹן גַּלָּיו
v'siftotéynu shévaḥ k'merḥavey rakí'a	וְשִׂפְתוֹתֵינוּ שֶׁבַח כְּמֶרְחֲבֵי רָקִיעַ
v'eynéynu m'irot kashémesh v'khayaré'aḥ	וְעֵינֵינוּ מְאִירוֹת כַּשֶּׁמֶשׁ וְכַיָּרֵחַ
v'yadéynu f'rusot k'nishrey shamáyim	וְיָדֵינוּ פְרוּשׂוֹת כְּנִשְׁרֵי שָׁמַיִם
v'ragléynu kalot ka'ayalot—	וְרַגְלֵינוּ קַלּוֹת כָּאַיָּלוֹת—
gam az, lo naspik l'hodot	גַּם אָז, לֹא נַסְפִּיק לְהוֹדוֹת
v'lu al p'li'ah aḥat	וְלוּ עַל פְּלִיאָה אַחַת
mini élef alfey alafim	מִנִּי אֶלֶף אַלְפֵי אֲלָפִים
v'ribey r'vavot.	וְרִבֵּי רְבָבוֹת.

מיוסד על תפילה מסורתית

HAL'LU: BEAUTY OF THE WORLD

Praise the world—
praise its fullness

and its longing,
its beauty and its grief.

Praise stone and fire,
lilac and river,

and the solitary bird
at the window.

Praise the moment
when the whole
bursts through pain

and the moment
when the whole
bursts forth in joy.

Praise the dying beauty
with all your breath,
and, praising, see

the beauty of the world
is your own.

THE FIRST WORD IN THIS POEM'S TITLE IS THE
HEBREW IMPERATIVE "PRAISE!"

HAL'LU: YIF'AT TEVEL

הַלְלוּ: יִפְעַת תֵּבֵל

Hal'lu et hatevel,
hal'lu et m'lo'ah.

הַלְלוּ אֶת הַתֵּבֵל,
הַלְלוּ אֶת מְלוֹאָהּ.

Hal'lu et kiséha,
et yofyah vigonah.

הַלְלוּ אֶת כִּסּוּפֶיהָ,
אֶת יָפְיָהּ וִיגוֹנָהּ.

Hal'lu éven va'esh,
nahar v'lilakh

הַלְלוּ אֶבֶן וָאֵשׁ,
נָהָר וְלֵילָךְ

v'tzipor bodedah
bahalon.

וְצִפּוֹר בּוֹדֵדָה
בַּחַלּוֹן.

Hal'lu et réga
p'ritzat hashalem

הַלְלוּ אֶת רֶגַע
פְּרִיצַת הַשָּׁלֵם

v'et réga
p'ritzat hashalem b'rinah.

וְאֶת רֶגַע
פְּרִיצַת הַשָּׁלֵם בְּרִנָּה.

Hal'lu b'khol m'odkhem
et hayófi hado'ekh—ur'u

הַלְלוּ בְּכָל מְאוֹדְכֶם
אֶת הַיְּפִי הַדּוֹעֵךְ—וּרְאוּ

ki yif'at hatevel
hi lakhem.

כִּי יִפְעַת הַתֵּבֵל
הִיא לָכֶם.

123

סעודת החג

THE FESTIVAL MEAL

רחצה

WASHING

ROḤTZAH

A PITCHER OF WATER, A BOWL, AND A TOWEL ARE PASSED AROUND
THE TABLE. WE WASH AND DRY OUR HANDS, AND SAY THE BLESSING.

WASHING THE HANDS

I will wash my palms
in innocence.

PSALM 26:6

Washing the hands,
we call to mind
the holiness of body.

נְטִילַת יָדַיִם

אֶרְחַץ בְּנִקָּיוֹן כַּפָּי.

תהלים כו:ו

תִּזְכֹּר נַפְשֵׁנוּ
אֶת קְדֻשַּׁת הַגוּף
בִּנְטִילַת יָדָיִם.

N'TILAT YADÁYIM

Erḥatz b'nikayon kapay.

PSALM 26:6

Tizkor nafshénu
et k'dushat haguf
bintilat yadáyim.

מוציאה / מצה

UNLEAVENED BREAD

MOTZI'AH / MATZAH

THE MEAL BEGINS WITH MATZAH. WE SAY THIS DOUBLE BLESSING
AND EAT.

BLESSING BEFORE THE MEAL,
BLESSING FOR EATING MATZAH

Bread is the sustenance of the heart.

PSALM 104:15

They baked unleavened cakes
from the dough they had taken out of Egypt;
it was not leavened
because they had been driven out of Egypt
and could not delay.

EXODUS 12:39

At this Festival of *Matzot*,
let us bless the source of life
that brings forth bread from the earth—

unleavened bread—
bread of affliction,

first taste
of our freedom.

בִּרְכַּת הַלֶּחֶם,
אֲכִילַת מַצָּה

וְלֶחֶם לְבַב־אֱנוֹשׁ יִסְעָד.

תהלים קד:טו

וַיֹּאפוּ אֶת־הַבָּצֵק
אֲשֶׁר הוֹצִיאוּ מִמִּצְרַיִם
עֻגֹת מַצּוֹת כִּי לֹא חָמֵץ
כִּי־גֹרְשׁוּ מִמִּצְרַיִם
וְלֹא יָכְלוּ לְהִתְמַהְמֵהַּ.

שמות יב:לט

BIRKAT HALÉHEM,
AKHILAT MATZAH

V'léhem l'vav-enosh yis'ad.

PSALM 104:15

Vayofu et-habatzek
asher hotzí'u mimitzráyim
ugot matzot ki lo hametz
ki-gor'shu mimitzráyim
v'lo yakh'lu l'hitmahmé'ah.

EXODUS 12:39

בְּחַג הַמַּצּוֹת הַזֶּה
נְבָרֵךְ אֶת עֵין הַחַיִּים
הַמּוֹצִיאָה לֶחֶם מִן הָאָרֶץ—

לֶחֶם עֹנִי—
טַעַם עַבְדוּתֵנוּ,

טְעִימָה רִאשׁוֹנָה
שֶׁל חֵרוּתֵנוּ.

B'hag hamatzot hazeh
n'varekh et eyn hahayim
hamotzí'ah léhem min ha'áretz—

léhem óni—
tá'am avduténu,

t'imah rishonah
shel heruténu.

129

מרור

BITTER HERB

MAROR

EARLIER IN THE SEDER, WE DIPPED THE SPRING VEGETABLE, *KARPAS*,
IN SALT WATER. NOW WE DIP THE BITTER HERB, *MAROR*, IN SWEET
ḤARÓSET. WE SAY THIS BLESSING, AND EAT.

DIPPING AND EATING
THE BITTER HERB

They made life bitter for them
with hard labor at mortar and brick
and with every kind of field work;
they drove them ruthlessly.

EXODUS 1:14

This bitterness—

taste of oppression,
taste of suffering,
taste of our torment.

טְבִילַת מָרוֹר
וַאֲכִילָתוֹ

וַיְמָרְרוּ אֶת־חַיֵּיהֶם
בַּעֲבֹדָה קָשָׁה בְּחֹמֶר וּבִלְבֵנִים
וּבְכָל־עֲבֹדָה בַּשָּׂדֶה
אֵת כָּל־עֲבֹדָתָם אֲשֶׁר־עָבְדוּ בָהֶם
בְּפָרֶךְ.

שמות א:יד

מָרוֹר זֶה—

טַעַם עָנְיֵנוּ,
טַעַם סִבְלֵנוּ,
טַעַם יִסּוּרֵינוּ.

T'VILAT MAROR
VA'AKHILATO

Vaymar'ru et-ḥayeyhem
ba'avodah kashah b'hómer uvilvenim
uvkhol-avodah basadeh
et kol-avodatam asher-av'du vahem
b'fárekh.

EXODUS 1:14

Maror zeh—

tá'am onyénu,
tá'am sivlénu,
tá'am yisuréynu.

סעודת החג

SWEET AND SALT, BITTER AND SWEET

Sweet: the newborn sprig,
greening

Salt: tears
hardening to rock

Salt: blood
rushing to the heart

Bitter: teeth
biting the earth

Bitter, side by side with *sweet*—
and the sweet becomes sweeter

Everything and its opposite,
unfolding

Life,
enfolding it all

כּוֹרֵךְ

SANDWICH

KOREKH

EATING THE "HILLEL SANDWICH"

WE PUT *MAROR* BETWEEN TWO PIECES OF MATZAH AND EAT THE
SANDWICH, THE ORIGIN OF WHICH IS CREDITED BY TRADITION TO
THE SAGE HILLEL. NO BLESSING IS SAID.

שׁוּלחָן עוֹרֵךְ
SETTING THE TABLE
SHULḤAN OREKH

THE MEAL IS SERVED

צפון

HIDDEN

TZAFUN

EATING THE *AFIKOMAN*

THE HIDDEN *AFIKOMAN* IS FOUND AND RETURNED TO THE LEADER
(SOMETIMES IN EXCHANGE FOR A REWARD). THE LEADER BREAKS
THE *AFIKOMAN* INTO PIECES AND DISTRIBUTES THEM TO ALL THE
PARTICIPANTS. THE MEAL, AND HENCE THE SEDER RITUAL, CAN ONLY
BE COMPLETED WHEN EACH PERSON EATS A PIECE.

CONCEALMENT AND REVEALMENT
KAVANAH

You desire truth about that which is hidden. Teach me wisdom about secret things.

PSALM 51:8

Children love treasure hunts. They like to search for hidden prizes as they discover and capture the world around them. Children also like to play hide-and-seek—the game of hiding from others.

Grown-ups, too, go on treasure hunts. What are the treasures we search for? Do we seek the gifts life might bestow on us? Do we look for what is hidden inside us?

Grown-ups also play hide-and-seek, hiding ourselves from others, sometimes even from ourselves. When do we play this game, and why?

We might find a clue in the child who cannot (will not?) ask. Why doesn't she speak? Is she shy? Fearful of criticism or humiliation? Or is her silence a way to shield herself, giving herself the room to ask her own questions, unhindered by the questions and answers of others?

Perhaps we too are seeking to uncover our own questions and find our own answers And perhaps each uncovering will contain the potential for discovery, bringing heightened awareness and making visible the breadth of our choices, the breadth of our freedom.

ברך

BLESSING

BAREKH

BLESSING AFTER THE MEAL

The earth will yield its fruit
and you shall eat your fill
and dwell securely on the land.

LEVITICUS 25:19

Grateful for the riches
of the good, giving earth,

we will tend the earth's gifts,
that they may flourish,

and seek sustenance for all
who dwell here with us.

בִּרְכַּת הַמָּזוֹן

וְנָתְנָה הָאָרֶץ פִּרְיָהּ
וַאֲכַלְתֶּם לָשֹׂבַע
וִישַׁבְתֶּם לָבֶטַח עָלֶיהָ.

ויקרא כה:יט

נוֹדֶה לְעֵין הַחַיִּים
הַזָּנָה אֶת הַכֹּל.

נִשְׁמֹר עַל הָאָרֶץ
הַטּוֹבָה וְהָרְחָבָה

וּנְבַקֵּשׁ שִׂבְעַת לֶחֶם
לְכָל הַדָּרִים בָּהּ.

BIRKAT HAMAZON

V'nat'nah ha'áretz piryah
va'akhaltem lasóvah
vishavtem lavétaḥ aléha.

LEVITICUS 25:19

Nodeh l'eyn haḥayim
hazanah et hakol.

Nishmor al ha'áretz
hatovah v'harḥavah

unvakesh siv'at léḥem
l'khol hadarim bah.

ברכת פרי הגפן

FRUIT OF THE VINE

BIRKAT P'RI HAGÉFEN

WE FILL THE WINE CUPS FOR THE THIRD TIME, SAY THIS BLESSING, AND DRINK.

FRUIT OF THE VINE

The mountains will drip wine
and all the hills will wave with grain.

AMOS 9:13

Let us bless the ever-flowing wellspring
that nourishes the fruit of the vine.

בִּרְכַּת פְּרִי הַגֶּפֶן

וְהִטְּיפוּ הֶהָרִים עָסִיס
וְכָל־הַגְּבָעוֹת תִּתְמוֹגַגְנָה.

עמוס ט:יג

נְבָרֵךְ אֶת הַמַּעְיָן הַשּׁוֹפֵעַ
הַמַּרְוֶה אֶת פְּרִי הַגֶּפֶן.

BIRKAT P'RI HAGÉFEN

*V'hitífu heharim asis
v'khol-hag'va'ot titmogágnah.*

AMOS 9:13

*N'varekh et hama'yan hashofé'a
hamarveh et p'ri hagéfen.*

סיום

CONCLUDING
THE SEDER

כוס אליהו

ELIJAH'S CUP

KOS ELIYÁHU

The rabbis of the Talmud held that the prophet Elijah might appear at the city gate in the guise of a beggar and that, in future times, he would come to us, bringing the Messiah. It has become customary in many communities to pour a fifth cup of wine at the seder for Elijah, and to open the door to invite him in. (The traditional fourth cup will be poured later in the seder, after *Hallel 2*.)

We welcome Elijah tonight, much as Abraham welcomed into his tent three strangers, whom the rabbis later declared to be angels.

THERE IS NO BLESSING FOR ELIJAH'S CUP, BUT THERE IS A RITUAL. WE FILL THE WINE CUPS, BUT WE DO NOT DRINK. WE EACH POUR A LITTLE OF OUR WINE INTO ELIJAH'S CUP. THEN WE OPEN THE DOOR TO INVITE HIM IN AND SING THE HEBREW WORDS TO THE TRADITIONAL MELODY.

Elijah the Prophet,
Elijah the Tishbite,
Elijah the Giladite.

Soon, in our days, may he come,
accompanied by the Messiah,
son of David.

אֵלִיָּהוּ הַנָּבִיא

אֵלִיָּהוּ הַנָּבִיא,
אֵלִיָּהוּ הַתִּשְׁבִּי,
אֵלִיָּהוּ הַגִּלְעָדִי.

בִּמְהֵרָה בְיָמֵינוּ
יָבוֹא אֵלֵינוּ
עִם מָשִׁיחַ בֶּן דָּוִד,
עִם מָשִׁיחַ בֶּן דָּוִד.

ELIYÁHU HANAVI

Eliyáhu hanavi,
eliyáhu hatishbi,
eliyáhu, eliyáhu, eliyáhu hagil'adi.

Bimherah v'yaméynu
yavo elénu
im mashí'aḥ ben david,
im mashí'aḥ ben david.

WHO WAS ELIJAH?
KAVANAH

In 1 Kings 19, the prophet Elijah walks forty days and forty nights into the wilderness, arriving at Horeb (Sinai), the mountain of God. He enters a cave and spends the night there. God calls to him, "Why are you here, Elijah? . . . Come out."

> And lo, God passed by. There was a great and mighty wind, splitting mountains and shattering rocks by the power of God; but God was not in the wind.

> After the wind—an earthquake; but God was not in the earthquake.

> After the earthquake—fire; but God was not in the fire.

> And after the fire—a voice of slender silence.

> . . . Then a voice addressed him: "Why are you here, Elijah?"

The story of the cave echoes the teachings that Moshe imparts to the Israelites in the wilderness, in Deuteronomy 30:11–14.

> Surely this commandment . . . is not too mysterious for you, nor is it far from you.

It is not in heaven, that you should say, "Who will go up to heaven for us and get it for us and let us hear it, so that we may do it?" Neither is it beyond the sea, that you should say, "Who will cross to the other side of the sea for us and get it for us and let us hear it, so that we may do it?"

For the thing is very close to you, in your mouth and in your heart, for you to do.

What voice do we hear? What is ours to fulfill and do? Is it time for us to take over Elijah's calling and work to bring about redemption?

THE PROMISE OF ELIJAH

We open the door to Elijah
and meet ourselves at the threshold.

May we find our callings here
to mend the broken world

and make whole
what is wounded and torn.

Soon—in our own time—

may healing blossom
in our hands.

הלל 2: מזמורי תהלים

PSALMS

HALLEL 2: MIZMOREY T'HILIM

WE SING VERSES EXCERPTED FROM PSALMS 114, 115, 117, AND 118 TO THE
TRADITIONAL MELODIES.

WHEN ISRAEL WENT FORTH

When Israel went forth from Egypt,
when the House of Jacob left
a people of foreign speech,

Judah became God's holy one,
Israel became God's dominion.

The sea saw and fled,
the Jordan River turned back.

The mountains leaped like rams;
the hills skipped like sheep.

PSALM 114:1–4

B'TZET YISRA'EL

B'tzet yisra'el mimitzráyim
bet ya'akov me'am lo'ez

hay'tah y'hudah l'kodsho
yisra'el mamsh'lotav.

Hayam ra'ah vayanos
hayarden yisov l'aḥor.

Heharim rak'du kh'eylim
g'va'ot kivney-tzon.

PSALM 114:1–4

בְּצֵאת יִשְׂרָאֵל

בְּצֵאת יִשְׂרָאֵל מִמִּצְרָיִם
בֵּית יַעֲקֹב מֵעַם לֹעֵז

הָיְתָה יְהוּדָה לְקָדְשׁוֹ
יִשְׂרָאֵל מַמְשְׁלוֹתָיו.

הַיָּם רָאָה וַיָּנֹס
הַיַּרְדֵּן יִסֹּב לְאָחוֹר.

הֶהָרִים רָקְדוּ כְאֵילִים
גְּבָעוֹת כִּבְנֵי־צֹאן.

תהלים קיד:א–ד

155

O SEA, WHAT ALARMS YOU

O sea, what alarms you
that you flee;
Jordan, that you turn back?

Why, O mountains,
do you leap like rams;
why, hills, do you skip like sheep?

Tremble, O earth,
at the presence of the Source,
at the presence of Jacob's Source,

which turns rock
into a pool of water,
stone into a flowing fountain.

PSALM 114:5–8

MAH-L'KHA HAYAM

מַה־לְּךָ הַיָּם

Mah-l'kha hayam ki tanus
hayarden tisov l'aḥor.

מַה־לְּךָ הַיָּם כִּי תָנוּס
הַיַּרְדֵּן תִּסֹּב לְאָחוֹר.

Heharim tirk'du kh'eylim
g'va'ot kivney-tzon.

הֶהָרִים תִּרְקְדוּ כְאֵילִים
גְּבָעוֹת כִּבְנֵי־צֹאן.

Milifney adon ḥuli áretz
milifney eló'ah ya'akov.

מִלִּפְנֵי אָדוֹן חוּלִי אָרֶץ
מִלִּפְנֵי אֱלוֹהַּ יַעֲקֹב.

Haḥof'khi hatzur agam-máyim
halamish l'may'no-máyim.

הַהֹפְכִי הַצּוּר אֲגַם־מָיִם
חַלָּמִישׁ לְמַעְיְנוֹ־מָיִם.

PSALM 114:5–8

תהלים קיד, ה–ח

157

MAY THE HOUSE OF ISRAEL BE BLESSED

May the House of Israel be blessed,
and the House of Aaron too.

May those in awe be blessed,
the little ones and the great ones.

May your numbers be increased—
yours and your children's too.

May you be blessed by the Creator
of heaven and earth.

The heavens belong to the Source of Life,
the earth belongs to people.

The dead cannot praise,
nor can those who descend into silence.

We shall praise the Source of Life
from now until eternity—

Hallelujah!

PSALM 115:12–18

Y'VAREKH ET-BET YISRA'EL

יְבָרֵךְ אֶת־בֵּית יִשְׂרָאֵל

Y'varekh et-bet yisra'el
y'varekh et-bet aharon.

יְבָרֵךְ אֶת־בֵּית יִשְׂרָאֵל
יְבָרֵךְ אֶת־בֵּית אַהֲרֹן.

Y'varekh yir'ey adonay
hak'tanim im-hag'dolim.

יְבָרֵךְ יִרְאֵי יְהֹוָה
הַקְּטַנִּים עִם־הַגְּדֹלִים.

Yosef adonay aleykhem
aleykhem v'al-b'neykhem.

יֹסֵף יְהֹוָה עֲלֵיכֶם
עֲלֵיכֶם וְעַל־בְּנֵיכֶם.

B'rukhim atem ladonay
osey shamáyim va'áretz.

בְּרוּכִים אַתֶּם לַיהֹוָה
עֹשֵׂה שָׁמַיִם וָאָרֶץ.

Hashamáyim shamáyim ladonay
v'ha'áretz natan livney-adam.

הַשָּׁמַיִם שָׁמַיִם לַיהֹוָה
וְהָאָרֶץ נָתַן לִבְנֵי־אָדָם.

Lo hametim y'hal'lu-yah
v'lo kol-yor'dey dumah.

לֹא הַמֵּתִים יְהַלְלוּ־יָהּ
וְלֹא כָּל־יֹרְדֵי דוּמָה.

Va'anáḥnu n'varekh yah
me'atah v'ad-olam—

וַאֲנַחְנוּ נְבָרֵךְ יָהּ
מֵעַתָּה וְעַד־עוֹלָם—

Hal'lu-yah!

הַלְלוּ־יָהּ.

PSALM 115:12–18

תהלים קטו, יב-יח

PRAISE GOD, ALL YOU NATIONS

Praise God, all you nations,
exalt God, all you peoples,

for great is God's kindness toward us
eternal is God's truth.
Hallelujah!

Praise God, for He is good,
for His kindness is eternal.

Let Israel declare
that His kindness is eternal.

Let the House of Aaron declare
His kindness is eternal.

Let those in awe of God declare
His kindness is eternal.

PSALMS 117:1–2; 118:1–4

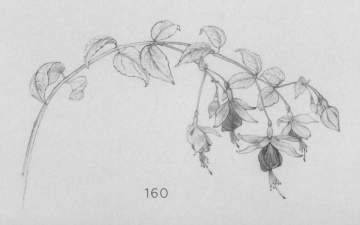

HAL'LU-ET ADONAY

הַלְלוּ־אֶת יְהוָה כָּל־גּוֹיִם

Hal'lu et-adonay kol-goyim
shab'húhu kol-ha'umim.

הַלְלוּ אֶת־יְהוָה כָּל־גּוֹיִם
שַׁבְּחוּהוּ כָּל־הָאֻמִּים.

Ki gavar aléynu ḥasdo
ve'emet-adonay l'olam.
Hal'lu-yah!

כִּי גָבַר עָלֵינוּ חַסְדּוֹ
וֶאֱמֶת־יְהוָה לְעוֹלָם.
הַלְלוּ־יָהּ!

Hodu ladonay ki-tov
ki l'olam ḥasdo.

הוֹדוּ לַיהוָה כִּי־טוֹב
כִּי לְעוֹלָם חַסְדּוֹ.

Yomar-na yisra'el
ki l'olam ḥasdo.

יֹאמַר־נָא יִשְׂרָאֵל
כִּי לְעוֹלָם חַסְדּוֹ.

Yom'ru-na vet-aharon
ki l'olam ḥasdo.

יֹאמְרוּ־נָא בֵית־אַהֲרֹן
כִּי לְעוֹלָם חַסְדּוֹ.

Yom'ru-na yir'ey adonay
ki l'olam ḥasdo.

יֹאמְרוּ־נָא יִרְאֵי יְהוָה
כִּי לְעוֹלָם חַסְדּוֹ.

PSALMS 117:1–2; 118:1–4

תהלים קיז, א–ב; קיח, א–ד

IN DISTRESS, I CALLED OUT

In distress, I called out to the Eternal One.
I was answered, my suffering allayed.

PSALM 118:5

THE VOICE OF REJOICING

The voice of rejoicing and salvation
resounds in the tents of the righteous.
The right hand of God will triumph.

PSALM 118:15

OPEN THE GATES OF JUSTICE

Open the gates of justice to me,
I will enter and give thanks to the Eternal One.

This is the gate to the Source of Life—
the righteous will enter here.

PSALM 118:19–20

MIN-HAMETZAR

מִן־הַמֵּצַר

Min-hametzar karáti yah
anáni vamerḥav yah.

מִן־הַמֵּצַר קָרָאתִי יָהּ
עֲנָנִי בַמֶּרְחָב יָהּ.

PSALM 118:5

תהלים קיח:ה

KOL RINAH VISHU'AH

קוֹל רִנָּה וִישׁוּעָה

Kol rinah vishu'ah
b'oholey tzadikim.
Y'min adonay ósah ḥáyil.

קוֹל רִנָּה וִישׁוּעָה
בְּאָהֳלֵי צַדִּיקִים.
יְמִין יְהוָה עֹשָׂה חָיִל.

PSALM 118:15

תהלים קיח:טו

PITḤU-LI SHA'AREY-TZÉDEK

פִּתְחוּ־לִי שַׁעֲרֵי־צֶדֶק

Pitḥu-li sha'arey-tzédek
avo-vam odeh yah.

פִּתְחוּ־לִי שַׁעֲרֵי־צֶדֶק
אָבֹא־בָם אוֹדֶה יָהּ.

Zeh-hashá'ar ladonay
tzadikim yavó'u vo.

זֶה־הַשַּׁעַר לַיהוָה
צַדִּיקִים יָבֹאוּ בוֹ.

PSALM 118:19–20

תהלים קיח:יט–כ

163

I GIVE THANKS

I give thanks, for You have answered
and redeemed me.

The rock rejected by the builders
has become the cornerstone.

Whatever comes from the Source of Life
is marvelous in our eyes.

This is the day God created—
let us delight and rejoice in it!

PSALM 118:21–24

OD'KHA KI ANITÁNI

אוֹדְךָ כִּי עֲנִיתָנִי

Od'kha ki anitáni
vat'hi-li lishu'ah.

אוֹדְךָ כִּי עֲנִיתָנִי
וַתְּהִי־לִי לִישׁוּעָה.

Éven ma'asu habonim
hay'tah l'rosh pinah.

אֶבֶן מָאֲסוּ הַבּוֹנִים
הָיְתָה לְרֹאשׁ פִּנָּה.

Me'et adonay hay'tah zot
hi niflat b'eynéynu.

מֵאֵת יְהוָה הָיְתָה זֹּאת
הִיא נִפְלָאת בְּעֵינֵינוּ.

Zeh-hayom asah adonay
nagílah v'nism'hah vo.

זֶה־הַיּוֹם עָשָׂה יְהוָה
נָגִילָה וְנִשְׂמְחָה בוֹ.

PSALM 118:21–24

תהלים קיח, כא–כד

ברכת פרי הגפן

FRUIT OF THE VINE

BIRKAT P'RI HAGÉFEN

WE FILL THE WINE CUPS FOR THE FOURTH TIME, SAY THIS BLESSING,
AND DRINK.

FRUIT OF THE VINE

Your vessels will overflow with young wine.

PROVERBS 3:10

Let us bless the ever-flowing wellspring
that nourishes fruit on the vine.

בִּרְכַּת פְּרִי הַגֶּפֶן

וְתִירוֹשׁ יְקָבֶיךָ יִפְרֹצוּ.

משלי ג:י

נְבָרֵךְ אֶת הַמַּעְיָן הַשׁוֹפֵעַ
הַמַּרְוֶה אֶת פְּרִי הַגֶּפֶן.

BIRKAT P'RI HAGÉFEN

V'tirosh y'kavékha yifrótzu.

PROVERBS 3:10

N'varekh et hama'yan hashofé'a
hamarveh et p'ri hagéfen.

נרצה

FULFILLMENT OF THE SEDER

NIRTZAH

We have arrived at *nirtzah*; we have fulfilled the seder ritual. But *nirtzah* is not the end; it is the completion of a stage. What will we bring with us into the world now that the seder is concluded?

FULFILLMENT YIELDS GRATEFULNESS. WE END THE EVENING WITH A CODA TO THE SEDER RITUAL.

BLESSING OF FRUITFULNESS

> I will provide the rain for your land in its seasons,
> the early rain and the late.
> You shall gather in your new grain
> and young wine and glowing oil.
> DEUTERONOMY 11:14

For the bountiful earth,
for the plenty of the field—

for seed to vine to bud,
for flower to fruit,
for grape to wine—

for the opening of our lives,
from enslavement to freedom
to fruition—

we give thanks.

בִּרְכַּת הַגֶּפֶן וּפִרְיָהּ

וְנָתַתִּי מְטַר־אַרְצְכֶם בְּעִתּוֹ
יוֹרֶה וּמַלְקוֹשׁ
וְאָסַפְתָּ דְגָנֶךָ
וְתִירֹשְׁךָ וְיִצְהָרֶךָ.
דברים יא:יד

BIRKAT HAGÉFEN UFIRYAH

V'natati m'tar-artz'khem b'ito
yoreh umalkosh
v'asafta d'ganékha
v'tirosh'kha v'yitzharékha.

DEUTERONOMY 11:14

עַל אֶרֶץ חֶמְדָּה וָשֶׁפַע,
עַל תְּנוּבַת הַשָּׂדֶה,

Al éretz ḥemdah vashéfa,
al t'nuvat hasadeh,

עַל זֶרַע, עַל גֶּפֶן וְנִצָּן,
עַל פֶּרַח וּפִרְיוֹ,

al zéra, al géfen v'nitzan,
al péraḥ ufiryo,

עַל עֲנָבִים
וְעַל הַיַּיִן,

al anavim
v'al hayáyin,

עַל הַמַּסָּע מֵעַבְדוּת
לְחֵרוּת וְלִשְׁלֵמוּת,

al hamasa me'avdut
l'ḥerut v'lishlemut,

רֵאשִׁית חַיֵּינוּ
כִּבְנוֹת וְכִבְנֵי חוֹרִין,

reshit ḥayéynu
kivnot v'khivney ḥorin,

נוֹדֶה וּנְבָרֵךְ.

nodeh unvarekh.

169

לַשָׁנָה הַבָּאָה בִּירוּשָׁלַיִם
שֶׁל צֶדֶק, שָׁלוֹם, וְאַחֲוָה

LASHANAH HABA'AH BIRUSHALÁYIM

SHEL TZÉDEK, SHALOM, V'AḤAVAH

NEXT YEAR MAY WE KNOW A JERUSALEM
OF JUSTICE, HARMONY, AND PEACE

שירים

SONGS

ABOUT THE SONGS

Following the conclusion of the seder proper, it is customary to sing game-like songs.

Ḥad Gadya is a song of accumulation: each line builds on and expands the previous one. *Ḥad Gadya* has been read as an allegory for the defeats of the many enemies and oppressors of the Hebrews.

Eḥad Mi Yodé'a is a numbers song. Our haggadah substitutes a female voice for the male voice in the opening lines of alternate stanzas. Thus, the first stanza opens *Eḥad mi yodé'a? Eḥad aní yodé'a* (the grammatically masculine form of "Who knows one? I know one") and the second stanza begins *Sh'náyim mi yodá'at? Sh'náyim ani yodá'at* (the grammatically feminine form of "Who knows two? I know two").

Adir Hu is an abecedarian (an alphabetic acrostic).

Karev Yom is another abecedarian, but only its final stanza is usually sung at the seder, and only that stanza is included here. Although the "game" is missing when one sings only a single stanza of *Karev Yom*, this is a song not to be missed: its words have a beautiful, mystical quality, and its melody is haunting.

ONE LITTLE KID

Ḥad gadya, ḥad gadya—
one little kid, one little kid
that my father bought for two zuzim.

First came the cat that ate the kid
that my father bought for two zuzim.

Then came the dog that bit the cat that ate the kid
that my father bought for two zuzim.

Then came the stick that beat the dog that bit the cat . . .

Then came the fire that burnt the stick that beat the dog . . .

Then came the water that quenched the fire . . .

Then came the ox that drank the water . . .

Then came the slaughterer that slew the ox . . .

Then came the Angel of Death who slew the slaughterer . . .

Then came the Holy One who slew the Angel of Death . . .

HAD GADYA / חַד גַּדְיָא

Had gadya, had gadya
dizvan aba bitrey zuzey.
Had gadya, had gadya.

חַד גַּדְיָא, חַד גַּדְיָא
דְּזַבֵּן אַבָּא בִּתְרֵי זוּזֵי.
חַד גַּדְיָא, חַד גַּדְיָא.

Va'ata shun'ra v'akhal l'gadya
dizvan aba bitrey zuzey.
Had gadya, had gadya.

וַאֲתָא שׁוּנְרָא וְאָכַל לְגַדְיָא
דְּזַבֵּן אַבָּא בִּתְרֵי זוּזֵי.
חַד גַּדְיָא, חַד גַּדְיָא.

Va'ata khalba v'nashakh l'shun'ra
d'akhal l'gadya
dizvan aba bitrey zuzey.
Had gadya, had gadya.

וַאֲתָא כַלְבָּא וְנָשַׁךְ לְשׁוּנְרָא
דְּאָכַל לְגַדְיָא
דְּזַבֵּן אַבָּא בִּתְרֵי זוּזֵי.
חַד גַּדְיָא, חַד גַּדְיָא.

Va'ata hutra v'hikah l'khalba
d'nashakh l'shun'ra d'akhal l'gadya
dizvan aba bitrey zuzey.
Had gadya, had gadya.

וַאֲתָא חוּטְרָא וְהִכָּה לְכַלְבָּא
דְּנָשַׁךְ לְשׁוּנְרָא דְּאָכַל לְגַדְיָא
דְּזַבֵּן אַבָּא בִּתְרֵי זוּזֵי.
חַד גַּדְיָא, חַד גַּדְיָא.

Va'ata nura v'saraf l'hutra
d'hikah l'khalba d'nashakh l'shun'ra
d'akhal l'gadya
dizvan aba bitrey zuzey.
Had gadya, had gadya.

וַאֲתָא נוּרָא וְשָׂרַף לְחוּטְרָא
דְּהִכָּה לְכַלְבָּא דְּנָשַׁךְ לְשׁוּנְרָא
דְּאָכַל לְגַדְיָא
דְּזַבֵּן אַבָּא בִּתְרֵי זוּזֵי.
חַד גַּדְיָא, חַד גַּדְיָא.

Va'ata maya v'chavah l'nura
d'saraf l'hutra, d'hikah l'khalba
d'nashakh l'shun'ra d'akhal l'gadya
dizvan aba bitrey zuzey.
Had gadya, had gadya.

וַאֲתָא מַיָּא וְכָבָה לְנוּרָא
דְּשָׂרַף לְחוּטְרָא דְּהִכָּה לְכַלְבָּא
דְּנָשַׁךְ לְשׁוּנְרָא דְּאָכַל לְגַדְיָא
דְּזַבֵּן אַבָּא בִּתְרֵי זוּזֵי.
חַד גַּדְיָא, חַד גַּדְיָא.

Va'ata tora v'shatah l'maya

וְאָתָא תוֹרָא וְשָׁתָה לְמַיָּא

d'chavah l'nura d'saraf l'hutra

דְּכָבָה לְנוּרָא דְּשָׂרַף לְחוּטְרָא

d'hikah l'khalba d'nashakh l'shun'ra

דְּהִכָּה לְכַלְבָּא דְּנָשַׁךְ לְשׁוּנְרָא

d'akhal l'gadya

דְּאָכַל לְגַדְיָא

dizvan aba bitrey zuzey.

דְּזַבַּן אַבָּא בִּתְרֵי זוּזֵי.

Ḥad gadya, ḥad gadya.

חַד גַּדְיָא, חַד גַּדְיָא.

Va'ata hashoḥet v'shaḥat l'tora

וְאָתָא הַשּׁוֹחֵט וְשָׁחַט לְתוֹרָא

d'shatah l'maya d'chavah l'nura

דְּשָׁתָה לְמַיָּא דְּכָבָה לְנוּרָא

d'saraf l'hutra d'hikah l'khalba

דְּשָׂרַף לְחוּטְרָא דְּהִכָּה לְכַלְבָּא

d'nashakh l'shun'ra d'akhal l'gadya

דְּנָשַׁךְ לְשׁוּנְרָא דְּאָכַל לְגַדְיָא

dizvan aba bitrey zuzey.

דְּזַבַּן אַבָּא בִּתְרֵי זוּזֵי.

Ḥad gadya, ḥad gadya.

חַד גַּדְיָא, חַד גַּדְיָא.

Va'ata malakh hamávet

וְאָתָא מַלְאַךְ הַמָּוֶת

v'shaḥat lashoḥet

וְשָׁחַט לַשּׁוֹחֵט

d'shaḥat l'tora d'shatah l'maya

דְּשָׁחַט לְתוֹרָא דְּשָׁתָה לְמַיָּא

d'chavah l'nura d'saraf l'ḥutra

דְּכָבָה לְנוּרָא דְּשָׂרַף לְחוּטְרָא

d'hikah l'khalba d'nashakh l'shun'ra

דְּהִכָּה לְכַלְבָּא דְּנָשַׁךְ לְשׁוּנְרָא

d'akhal l'gadya

דְּאָכַל לְגַדְיָא

dizvan aba bitrey zuzey.

דְּזַבַּן אַבָּא בִּתְרֵי זוּזֵי.

Ḥad gadya, ḥad gadya.

חַד גַּדְיָא, חַד גַּדְיָא.

Va'ata hakadosh barukh hu

וְאָתָא הַקָּדוֹשׁ בָּרוּךְ הוּא

v'shaḥat l'malakh hamávet

וְשָׁחַט לְמַלְאַךְ הַמָּוֶת

d'shaḥat lashoḥet d'shaḥat l'tora

דְּשָׁחַט לַשּׁוֹחֵט דְּשָׁחַט לְתוֹרָא

d'shatah l'maya d'chavah l'nura

דְּשָׁתָה לְמַיָּא דְּכָבָה לְנוּרָא

d'saraf l'ḥutra d'hikah l'khalba

דְּשָׂרַף לְחוּטְרָא דְּהִכָּה לְכַלְבָּא

d'nashakh l'shun'ra d'akhal l'gadya

דְּנָשַׁךְ לְשׁוּנְרָא דְּאָכַל לְגַדְיָא

dizvan aba bitrey zuzey.

דְּזַבַּן אַבָּא בִּתְרֵי זוּזֵי.

Ḥad gadya, ḥad gadya.

חַד גַּדְיָא, חַד גַּדְיָא.

EHAD MI YODÉ'A?

Ehad mi yodé'a? Ehad ani yodé'a.
Ehad elohéynu shebashamáyim uva'áretz.

Sh'náyim, mi yodá'at? Sh'náyim ani yodá'at.
Sh'ney luhot hab'rit.
Ehad elohéynu shebashamáyim uva'áretz.

Sh'loshah mi yodé'a? Sh'loshah ani yodé'a.
Sh'loshah avot.
Sh'ney luhot hab'rit.
Ehad elohéynu shebashamáyim uva'áretz.

Arba mi yodá'at? Arba ani yodá'at.
Arba imahot.
Sh'loshah avot.
Sh'ney luhot hab'rit.
Ehad elohéynu shebashamáyim uva'áretz.

Hamishah mi yodé'a? Hamishah ani yodé'a.
Hamishah humshey torah.
Arba imahot.
Sh'loshah avot.
Sh'ney luhot hab'rit.
Ehad elohéynu shebashamáyim uva'áretz.

Shishah mi yodá'at? Shishah ani yodá'at.
Shishah sidrey mishnah.
Hamishah humshey torah.
Arba imahot.

אֶחָד מִי יוֹדֵעַ?

אֶחָד מִי יוֹדֵעַ? אֶחָד אֲנִי יוֹדֵעַ.
אֶחָד אֱלֹהֵינוּ שֶׁבַּשָּׁמַיִם וּבָאָרֶץ.

שְׁנַיִם מִי יָדַעַת? שְׁנַיִם אֲנִי יָדַעַת.
שְׁנֵי לוּחוֹת הַבְּרִית.
אֶחָד אֱלֹהֵינוּ שֶׁבַּשָּׁמַיִם וּבָאָרֶץ.

שְׁלֹשָׁה מִי יוֹדֵעַ? שְׁלֹשָׁה אֲנִי יוֹדֵעַ.
שְׁלֹשָׁה אָבוֹת.
שְׁנֵי לוּחוֹת הַבְּרִית.
אֶחָד אֱלֹהֵינוּ שֶׁבַּשָּׁמַיִם וּבָאָרֶץ.

אַרְבַּע מִי יָדַעַת? אַרְבַּע אֲנִי יָדַעַת.
אַרְבַּע אִמָּהוֹת.
שְׁלֹשָׁה אָבוֹת.
שְׁנֵי לוּחוֹת הַבְּרִית.
אֶחָד אֱלֹהֵינוּ שֶׁבַּשָּׁמַיִם וּבָאָרֶץ.

חֲמִשָּׁה מִי יוֹדֵעַ? חֲמִשָּׁה אֲנִי יוֹדֵעַ.
חֲמִשָּׁה חוּמְשֵׁי תוֹרָה.
אַרְבַּע אִמָּהוֹת.
שְׁלֹשָׁה אָבוֹת.
שְׁנֵי לוּחוֹת הַבְּרִית.
אֶחָד אֱלֹהֵינוּ שֶׁבַּשָּׁמַיִם וּבָאָרֶץ.

שִׁשָּׁה מִי יָדַעַת? שִׁשָּׁה אֲנִי יָדַעַת.
שִׁשָּׁה סִדְרֵי מִשְׁנָה.
חֲמִשָּׁה חוּמְשֵׁי תוֹרָה.
אַרְבַּע אִמָּהוֹת.

Sh'loshah avot.

Sh'ney luḥot hab'rit.

Eḥad elohéynu shebashamáyim uva'áretz.

Shiv'ah mi yodé'a? Shivah ani yodé'a.

Shiv'ah y'mey shab'ta.

Shishah sidrey mishnah.

Ḥamishah ḥumshey torah.

Arba imahot.

Sh'loshah avot.

Sh'ney luḥot hab'rit.

Eḥad elohéynu shebashamáyim uva'áretz.

Sh'monah mi yodá'at? Sh'monah ani yodá'at.

Sh'monah y'mey milah.

Shiv'ah y'mey shab'ta.

Shishah sidrey mishnah.

Ḥamishah ḥumshey torah.

Arba imahot.

Sh'loshah avot.

Sh'ney luḥot hab'rit.

Eḥad elohéynu shebashamáyim uva'áretz.

Tish'ah mi yodé'a? Tish'ah ani yodé'a.

Tish'ah yarḥey ledah.

Sh'monah y'mey milah.

Shiv'ah y'mey shab'ta.

Shishah sidrey mishnah.

Ḥamishah ḥumshey torah.

Arba imahot.

Sh'loshah avot.

שְׁלֹשָׁה אָבוֹת.
שְׁנֵי לוּחוֹת הַבְּרִית.
אֶחָד אֱלֹהֵינוּ שֶׁבַּשָּׁמַיִם וּבָאָרֶץ.

שִׁבְעָה מִי יוֹדֵעַ? שִׁבְעָה אֲנִי יוֹדֵעַ.
שִׁבְעָה יְמֵי שַׁבְּתָא.
שִׁשָּׁה סִדְרֵי מִשְׁנָה.
חֲמִשָּׁה חוּמְשֵׁי תוֹרָה.
אַרְבַּע אִמָּהוֹת.
שְׁלֹשָׁה אָבוֹת.
שְׁנֵי לוּחוֹת הַבְּרִית.
אֶחָד אֱלֹהֵינוּ שֶׁבַּשָּׁמַיִם וּבָאָרֶץ.

שְׁמוֹנָה מִי יֵדַעַת? שְׁמוֹנָה אֲנִי יֵדַעַת.
שְׁמוֹנָה יְמֵי מִילָה.
שִׁבְעָה יְמֵי שַׁבְּתָא.
שִׁשָּׁה סִדְרֵי מִשְׁנָה.
חֲמִשָּׁה חוּמְשֵׁי תוֹרָה.
אַרְבַּע אִמָּהוֹת
שְׁלֹשָׁה אָבוֹת.
שְׁנֵי לוּחוֹת הַבְּרִית.
אֶחָד אֱלֹהֵינוּ שֶׁבַּשָּׁמַיִם וּבָאָרֶץ.

תִּשְׁעָה מִי יוֹדֵעַ? תִּשְׁעָה אֲנִי יוֹדֵעַ.
תִּשְׁעָה יַרְחֵי לֵידָה.
שְׁמוֹנָה יְמֵי מִילָה.
שִׁבְעָה יְמֵי שַׁבְּתָא.
שִׁשָּׁה סִדְרֵי מִשְׁנָה.
חֲמִשָּׁה חוּמְשֵׁי תוֹרָה.
אַרְבַּע אִמָּהוֹת
שְׁלֹשָׁה אָבוֹת.

Sh'ney luḥot hab'rit.
Eḥad elohéynu shebashamáyim uva'áretz.

Asarah mi yodá'at? Asarah ani yodá'at.
Asarah dib'raya.
Tish'ah yarḥey ledah.
Sh'monah y'mey milah.
Shiv'ah y'mey shab'ta.
Shishah sidrey mishnah.
Ḥamishah ḥumshey torah.
Arba imahot.
Sh'loshah avot.
Sh'ney luḥot hab'rit.
Eḥad elohéynu shebashamáyim uva'áretz.

Aḥad asar mi yodé'a? Aḥad asar ani yodé'a.
Aḥad asar kokh'vaya.
Asarah dib'raya.
Tish'ah yarḥey ledah.
Sh'monah y'mey milah.
Shiv'ah y'mey shab'ta.
Shishah sidrey mishnah.
Ḥamishah ḥumshey torah.
Arba imahot.
Sh'loshah avot.
Sh'ney luḥot hab'rit.
Eḥad elohéynu shebashamáyim uva'áretz.

Sh'neym asar mi yodá'at? Sh'neym asar ani yodá'at.
Sh'neym asar shivtaya.
Aḥad asar kokh'vaya.

שְׁנֵי לוּחוֹת הַבְּרִית.
אֶחָד אֱלֹהֵינוּ שֶׁבַּשָּׁמַיִם וּבָאָרֶץ.

עֲשָׂרָה מִי יוֹדֵעַת? עֲשָׂרָה אֲנִי יוֹדַעַת.
עֲשָׂרָה דִבְּרַיָּא.
תִּשְׁעָה יַרְחֵי לֵידָה.
שְׁמוֹנָה יְמֵי מִילָה.
שִׁבְעָה יְמֵי שַׁבְּתָא.
שִׁשָּׁה סִדְרֵי מִשְׁנָה.
חֲמִשָּׁה חוּמְשֵׁי תוֹרָה.
אַרְבַּע אִמָּהוֹת
שְׁלֹשָׁה אָבוֹת.
שְׁנֵי לוּחוֹת הַבְּרִית.
אֶחָד אֱלֹהֵינוּ שֶׁבַּשָּׁמַיִם וּבָאָרֶץ.

אַחַד עָשָׂר מִי יוֹדֵעַ? אַחַד עָשָׂר אֲנִי יוֹדֵעַ.
אַחַד עָשָׂר כּוֹכְבַיָּא.
עֲשָׂרָה דִבְּרַיָּא.
תִּשְׁעָה יַרְחֵי לֵידָה.
שְׁמוֹנָה יְמֵי מִילָה.
שִׁבְעָה יְמֵי שַׁבְּתָא.
שִׁשָּׁה סִדְרֵי מִשְׁנָה.
חֲמִשָּׁה חוּמְשֵׁי תוֹרָה.
אַרְבַּע אִמָּהוֹת
שְׁלֹשָׁה אָבוֹת.
שְׁנֵי לוּחוֹת הַבְּרִית.
אֶחָד אֱלֹהֵינוּ שֶׁבַּשָּׁמַיִם וּבָאָרֶץ.

שְׁנֵים עָשָׂר מִי יוֹדֵעַת? שְׁנֵים עָשָׂר אֲנִי יוֹדַעַת.
שְׁנֵים עָשָׂר שִׁבְטַיָּא.
אַחַד עָשָׂר כּוֹכְבַיָּא.

Asarah dib'raya.

Tish'ah yarḥey ledah.

Sh'monah y'mey milah.

Shiv'ah y'mey shab'ta.

Shishah sidrey mishnah.

Ḥamishah ḥumshey torah.

Arba imahot.

Sh'loshah avot.

Sh'ney luḥot hab'rit.

Eḥad elohéynu shebashamáyim uva'áretz.

Sh'loshah asar mi yodé'a? Sh'loshah asar ani yodé'a.

Sh'loshah asar midaya.

Sh'neym asar shivtaya.

Aḥad asar kokh'vaya.

Asarah dib'raya.

Tish'ah yarḥey ledah.

Sh'monah y'mey milah.

Shiv'ah y'mey shab'ta.

Shishah sidrey mishnah.

Ḥamishah ḥumshey torah.

Arba imahot.

Sh'loshah avot.

Sh'ney luḥot hab'rit.

Eḥad elohéynu shebashamáyim uva'áretz.

עֲשָׂרָה דִבְּרַיָּא.
תִּשְׁעָה יַרְחֵי לֵידָה.
שְׁמוֹנָה יְמֵי מִילָה.
שִׁבְעָה יְמֵי שַׁבַּתָּא.
שִׁשָּׁה סִדְרֵי מִשְׁנָה.
חֲמִשָּׁה חוּמְשֵׁי תוֹרָה.
אַרְבַּע אִמָּהוֹת
שְׁלֹשָׁה אָבוֹת.
שְׁנֵי לוּחוֹת הַבְּרִית.
אֶחָד אֱלֹהֵינוּ שֶׁבַּשָּׁמַיִם וּבָאָרֶץ.

שְׁלֹשָׁה עָשָׂר מִי יוֹדֵעַ? שְׁלֹשָׁה עָשָׂר אֲנִי יוֹדֵעַ.
שְׁלֹשָׁה עָשָׂר מִדַּיָּא.
שְׁנֵים עָשָׂר שִׁבְטַיָּא.
אַחַד עָשָׂר כּוֹכְבַיָּא.
עֲשָׂרָה דִבְּרַיָּא.
תִּשְׁעָה יַרְחֵי לֵידָה.
שְׁמוֹנָה יְמֵי מִילָה.
שִׁבְעָה יְמֵי שַׁבַּתָּא.
שִׁשָּׁה סִדְרֵי מִשְׁנָה.
חֲמִשָּׁה חוּמְשֵׁי תוֹרָה.
אַרְבַּע אִמָּהוֹת
שְׁלֹשָׁה אָבוֹת.
שְׁנֵי לוּחוֹת הַבְּרִית.
אֶחָד אֱלֹהֵינוּ שֶׁבַּשָּׁמַיִם וּבָאָרֶץ.

WHO KNOWS ONE?

Who knows one? I know one!
One is our God in heaven and on earth.

Who knows two? I know two!
Two are the tablets of the covenant,
one is our God in heaven and on earth.

Who knows three? I know three!
Three are the forefathers,
two are the tablets of the covenant,
one is our God in heaven and on earth.

Who knows four? I know four!
Four are the foremothers . . .

Who knows five? I know five!
Five are the books of the Torah . . .

Who knows six? I know six!
Six are the orders of the Mishnah . . .

Who knows seven? I know seven!
Seven are the days of the week . . .

Who knows eight? I know eight!
Eight are the days until circumcision . . .

Who knows nine? I know nine!
Nine are the months of pregnancy . . .

Who knows ten? I know ten!
Ten are the Commandments . . .

Who knows eleven? I know eleven!
Eleven are the stars in Joseph's dream . . .

Who knows twelve? I know twelve!
Twelve are the tribes of Israel . . .

Who knows thirteen? I know thirteen!
Thirteen are the attributes of God . . .

MIGHTY IS GOD

Mighty is God, mighty is God.
May He build the Temple soon,
speedily, in our days.
O God, build your Temple speedily.

Chosen is He, great is He, eminent is He.
May He build the Temple soon,
speedily, in our days.
O God, build your Temple speedily.

Glorious is He, ancient is He, just is He.
May He build the Temple soon . . .

Kind is He, pure is He, unique is He.
May He build the Temple soon . . .

Powerful is He, learned is He, kingly is He.
May He build the Temple soon . . .

Awesome is He, strong is He, heroic is He.
May He build the Temple soon . . .

Redeeming is He, righteous is He, holy is He.
May He build the Temple soon . . .

Compassionate is He, almighty is He, strong is He.
May He build the Temple soon . . .

ADIR HU

אַדִּיר הוּא

Adir hu, Adir hu,	אַדִּיר הוּא, אַדִּיר הוּא,
yivneh veto b'karov,	יִבְנֶה בֵיתוֹ בְּקָרוֹב,
bimherah bimherah,	בִּמְהֵרָה בִּמְהֵרָה
b'yaméynu b'karov.	בְּיָמֵינוּ בְּקָרוֹב.
El b'ney, el b'ney,	אֵל בְּנֵה, אֵל בְּנֵה,
b'ney vetkha b'karov.	בְּנֵה בֵיתְךָ בְּקָרוֹב.

Baḥur hu, Gadol hu, Dagul hu,	בָּחוּר הוּא, גָּדוֹל הוּא, דָּגוּל הוּא
yivneh veto b'karov,	יִבְנֶה בֵיתוֹ בְּקָרוֹב,
bimherah bimherah,	בִּמְהֵרָה בִּמְהֵרָה
b'yaméynu b'karov.	בְּיָמֵינוּ בְּקָרוֹב.
El b'ney, el b'ney,	אֵל בְּנֵה, אֵל בְּנֵה,
b'ney vetkha b'karov.	בְּנֵה בֵיתְךָ בְּקָרוֹב.

Hadur hu, Vatik hu, Zakay hu	הָדוּר הוּא, וָתִיק הוּא, זַכַּאי הוּא
yivneh veto b'karov . . .	יִבְנֶה בֵיתוֹ בְּקָרוֹב . . .

Ḥasid hu, Tahor hu, Yaḥid hu	חָסִיד הוּא, טָהוֹר הוּא, יָחִיד הוּא
yivneh veto b'karov . . .	יִבְנֶה בֵיתוֹ בְּקָרוֹב . . .

Kabir hu, Lamud hu, Mélekh hu	כַּבִּיר הוּא, לָמוּד הוּא, מֶלֶךְ הוּא
yivneh veto b'karov . . .	יִבְנֶה בֵיתוֹ בְּקָרוֹב . . .

Nora hu, Sagiv hu, Izuz hu	נוֹרָא הוּא, סַגִּיב הוּא, עִזּוּז הוּא
yivneh veto b'karov . . .	יִבְנֶה בֵיתוֹ בְּקָרוֹב . . .

Podeh hu, TZadik hu, Kadosh hu	פּוֹדֶה הוּא, צַדִּיק הוּא, קָדוֹשׁ הוּא
yivneh veto b'karov . . .	יִבְנֶה בֵיתוֹ בְּקָרוֹב . . .

Raḥum hu, Shaday hu, Takif hu	רַחוּם הוּא, שַׁדַּי הוּא, תַּקִּיף הוּא
yivneh veto b'karov . . .	יִבְנֶה בֵיתוֹ בְּקָרוֹב . . .

BRING NEAR THE DAY

Bring near the day
that is neither day nor night.

Proclaim that the day
and the night are Yours.

Place sentries to watch over Your city
all day and all night.

Make the dark of night as bright
as the light of day.

KAREV YOM

קָרֶב יוֹם

Karev yom, karev yom
asher hu lo yom v'lo láylah.

קָרֶב יוֹם, קָרֶב יוֹם
אֲשֶׁר הוּא לֹא יוֹם וְלֹא לַיְלָה.

Ram hoda, hoda, hoda,
ki l'kha hayom af l'kha haláylah.

רָם הוֹדַע, הוֹדַע, הוֹדַע,
כִּי לְךָ הַיּוֹם אַף לְךָ הַלַּיְלָה.

Shomrim hafked, hafked l'irkha
kol hayom v'khol haláylah.

שׁוֹמְרִים הַפְקֵד, הַפְקֵד לְעִירְךָ
כָּל הַיּוֹם וְכָל הַלַּיְלָה.

Ta'ir k'or yom ḥeshkhat láylah
váyhi baḥatzi haláylah.

תָּאִיר כְּאוֹר יוֹם חֶשְׁכַת לַיְלָה
וַיְהִי בַּחֲצִי הַלַּיְלָה.

ACKNOWLEDGMENTS

כּוֹסִי רְוָיָה *(kosi r'vayah)*—once again, my cup runneth over. Where do I begin to thank my angels?

I begin with the beginning. Nancy Augustus is more than a friend and far more than a donor. What words can describe or adequately thank someone who urged this haggadah into being before it was a glimmer in the author's eye and encouraged it—believed in it—at every stage? Nancy's generous funding, and her time spent fundraising, kept me going through the thick and thin of it and sustained me in every way.

Other funders include the Hadassah-Brandeis Institute, which over the years has supported the research and writing of a number of my books, including this one. I thank the Institute for its ongoing faith in me.

The Mordecai M. Kaplan Center, under the direction of Daniel Cedarbaum *z"l*, underwrote production costs for *Night of Beginnings*. I am honored to be associated with an institution named for Rabbi Kaplan, the founder of Reconstructionist Judaism.

Alongside necessary financial support, other kinds of sustenance are crucial for fulfilling an author's aims. Yair Zakovitch, Bible scholar, poet, and friend of half a century, not only shared with me his profound knowledge of, and original perspectives on, biblical texts but poetically refined my Hebrew blessings. Yair enhanced this book greatly, and I am deeply grateful for his dedication to this project—and to all my work.

I benefited greatly from the expertise of liturgy scholar Richard Sarason. Rick reviewed multiple drafts of the manuscript and, through ongoing correspondence, provided a wealth of scholarly knowledge that enriched the comments accompanying much of the liturgy.

Suzanne Singer and Judith Plaskow read and responded to early drafts of the manuscript. Their questions and insightful observations helped focus and move the project along.

Stephen Damon *z"l* inspired me with his unique perspective on the haggadah themes and, over the course of more than a decade, engaged me in discussion of subjects such as exodus and exile. I wish Stephen could be here to see what emerged out of our many conversations.

Conversation: the blessing of friendship. I have indeed been blessed with many other loving friends who offered their thoughts about the Exodus story, the haggadah, and related topics before the book was even in its first draft. Had I another book's worth of pages, I would describe each individual's gift to me. As it is, I have to settle for this list, with hope that each person will hear my appreciation. They are: David Biale, Lucille Lang Day, Natan Fenner, Yael Heffer, Naamah Kelman, Karen Leo, Beth Lieberman, Hava Ratinsky, Mel Scult, and Claire Sherman.

I am grateful to the Jewish Publication Society and its editors, Barry Schwartz and Joy Weinberg, and to the editors and staff of the University of Nebraska Press, who partnered to bring this book to the reading public.

In creating this haggadah, I had the unusual opportunity to perform many of the roles of production editor, a labor-intensive but rewarding task, and I was fortunate to have a great team of professionals to work with—beginning with my longtime editor Bronwyn Becker.

It is hard to imagine a more gifted, sensitive, and dedicated editor than Bronwyn. I will never be able to thank her enough for her many brilliant insights and the countless hours she devoted to this book.

The talented designer Rachelle Vagy collaborated with me to realize my vision of הִדּוּר מִצְוָה (*hiddur mitzvah*)—the aesthetic enhancement of religious ritual—producing a lyrical and inviting haggadah. Rachelle's wonderful sense of color added a special element of beauty.

Three experts in Hebrew language made essential contributions: David Harband, the *nakdan*, inserted the diacritics into the Hebrew texts; Bible scholar Daniel Fisher provided transliterations; David E. S. Stein, scholar of Bible and Judaica, reviewed the biblical Hebrew citations and served as the final Hebrew proofreader.

And then there is Steven Rood—not part of any list—magnificent poet, critical reader, spouse, co-parent, and best friend. During long days of the coronavirus lockdown, Steve and I sat together in our sunny little "reading room," researching and studying the Book of Exodus, delving into the history of haggadot, and discussing every bit of this haggadah. As I have said before and cannot say better today, Steve is my *without whom not*, and I thank him for it all.

Publication of *Night of Beginnings* is made possible by the vision and generosity of the Mordecai M. Kaplan Center for Jewish Peoplehood.

The mission of the Mordecai M. Kaplan Center for Jewish Peoplehood is to disseminate and promote the thought and writings of Rabbi Kaplan and to advance the cross-denominational agenda of the Kaplanian approach to Judaism in the twenty-first century. This mission is fulfilled in the following ways: by producing, or otherwise making widely available, publications and other resources in print and online; by facilitating academic conferences and broader educational events; and by spurring creative experimentation in the formation or reorganization of Jewish communities and institutions. In so doing, we strive to ensure that the influence of Rabbi Kaplan's thought in the twenty-first century is commensurate with his stature as one of the two or three most influential Jewish thinkers of the twentieth century. Visit www.kaplancenter.org for more information.

In true Kaplanian spirit, with a boldly original approach to Jewish traditions old and new, *Night of Beginnings* carries Jewish prayer and theology forward into our times. We are honored to support this work.

ABOUT THE AUTHOR

As a poet, translator, liturgist, and artist, Marcia Falk has pursued a lifelong commitment to beauty, meaning, and the connection between them. Her theology and approach to creating new liturgy have evolved over the past four decades and become less easy to categorize—even for herself. As her work has matured, she has found growing freedom in the ways she expresses this central commitment.

Known widely for her groundbreaking prayer books, *The Book of Blessings* and *The Days Between*, which re-create Hebrew and English prayer from an inclusive, nonpatriarchal perspective, Falk is also the creator of a volume combining her art and poetry, *Inner East: Illuminated Poems and Blessings*, and other books of poetry and translation.

Falk received a bachelor's in philosophy from Brandeis University and a doctorate in English and comparative literature from Stanford. She was a Fulbright Scholar in Bible and Hebrew literature at the Hebrew University of Jerusalem and, later, a postdoctoral fellow. For two decades she was a university professor. A painter and Life Member of the Art Students League, she has exhibited her artwork internationally.

Falk lives in Berkeley, California, with her spouse, poet Steven Rood. Their son, Abraham Gilead Falk-Rood, teaches high school English to new immigrants.

Falk's book titles and art may be viewed at www.marciafalk.com.

Author photo by Brian Miller

The English portions of *Night of Beginnings* were set in Baskerville and Metropolis. John Baskerville designed his eponymous serif typeface in the 1750s. It was intended as a refinement of what are now called old-style typefaces of the period, especially those of William Caslon.

Metropolis is a modern, geometric sans serif typeface created by Chris Simpson in 2018. Clean and high-contrast, it was designed for optimal readability.

The Hebrew portions of the book were set in Days and Nights, a calligraphy-based typeface created by Ben Nathan in 2013, when he was a student at the Bezalel Academy of Art and Design in Jerusalem. He lives in Tel Aviv and has established his own type foundry, Hafontia.

From Marcia Falk—acclaimed poet, artist, and author of *The Book of Blessings* and *The Days Between*—comes a groundbreaking haggadah that presents the Exodus narrative in its entirety and highlights the actions of its female characters. Falk's thought-provoking commentaries invite us to bring personal reflections to the story; her revolutionary blessings, in Hebrew and English, offer a nonpatriarchal vision of the divine; and her *kavanot*—meditative directions for prayer—introduce a new genre to the seder ritual. The author's lyrical drawings unite the varied elements of this elegant haggadah.

Night of Beginnings once more reveals the liturgical genius of Marcia Falk. Her blessings honor classical Jewish tradition while celebrating a modern ethos that is feminist and inclusive. This magnificent haggadah will provide a spiritually enriching seder experience of unique depth.

—RABBI DAVID ELLENSON, Chancellor Emeritus, Hebrew Union College–
Jewish Institute of Religion

How lovely to have a haggadah that makes central the biblical narrative that hovers over—but is absent from—the traditional haggadah. Those familiar with Marcia Falk's transformational work on Jewish blessings will be delighted by her new blessings for all parts of the seder, while those not yet acquainted with her blessings will find them a revelation. This is a beautiful haggadah.

—JUDITH PLASKOW, author of *Standing Again at Sinai* and co-author with
Carol P. Christ of *Goddess and God in the World*

Poet and scholar Marcia Falk builds a luminous bridge between the old and the new, firmly mooring the modern ritual to the ancient biblical narrative and inspiring us with the preeminent story of the passage from slavery to freedom, from darkness to light.

—YAIR ZAKOVITCH, Emeritus Professor of Bible, the Hebrew University
of Jerusalem, and recipient of the Israel Prize

The Jewish Publication Society
Philadelphia PA 19103-1399
jps.org

ISBN 978-0-8276-1551-9   US $19.95

51995

9 780827 615519